François Truffaut

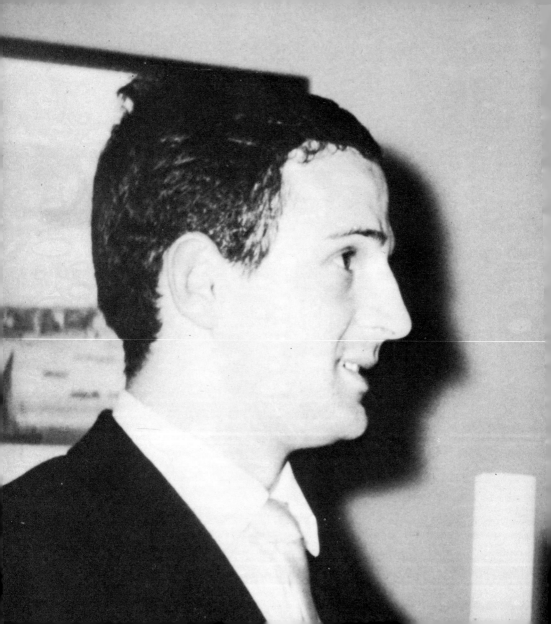

François Truffaut

C. G. Crisp

Praeger

BOOKS THAT MATTER

*Published in the United States of America in 1972
by Praeger Publishers, Inc.
111 Fourth Avenue, New York, N.Y. 10003.*

*Library of Congress Catalog Card Number:
75-151834*

Produced by November Books Limited

Printed in Great Britain

*Stills by courtesy of Columbia-Warner, Connois-
seur, Contemporary, Les Films du Carrosse, Gala,
National Film Archive, Rank Film Distributors,
20th Century-Fox, United Artists.*

Contents

Introduction

'What is direction? The sum total of the decisions taken in the course of the preparation, the filming, and the putting together of a film; it seems to me that all the choices that confront a director – of scenario, of ellipses, of locations, collaborators, actors, angles of view, lenses, of takes to be printed, of soundtrack and of music – enforce on him a number of concrete *decisions*, and what is called direction is obviously the common tendency of the thousands of decisions made in the course of six, nine, twelve or sixteen months of work. That's why "partial" directors – those who only deal with one stage of all that – however talented they are, interest me less than Bergman, Buñuel, Hitchcock and Welles, who *are* completely their films.'

The aim of this book is to specify the nature of the decisions taken by Truffaut in the course of his career, together with the motives that have guided them. It is right to approach his films in a meticulous, factual manner, since he clearly does so himself, as is apparent from the lack of pretension and of mystification both in his book on Alfred Hitchcock and in his discussion of his own work. He sees himself first and foremost as a craftsman rather than as an artist, manipulating certain basic materials in simple and clearly definable ways. He has never been secretive about this creative process: over the years, in many interviews, he has conscientiously described the process by which each of his films came to be made. It is on these interviews that the following discussions are based.

This might seem a very modest aim, but it is a justifiable one as most of these interviews were published only in French-language magazines of modest circulation. However, any criticism of Truffaut's films ought to start by taking into account the conditions in which they were originally conceived. This is particularly rewarding in the case of the films which were less successful with the public, such as *Tirez sur le pianiste, La Peau Douce, Fahrenheit 451* and *La Sirène du Mississippi,* which need to be approached with some awareness of Truffaut's background and personality, and some appreciation of his intentions, which are not always immediately obvious.

Wherever he has stated the relevant facts simply and concisely, I have not thought it necessary to pretend that the words are other than his; where he has repeatedly discussed them, in different terms and with different emphases, I have summarised the trend of his arguments as concisely as possible. On the few occasions when he has not, to my knowledge, specified motives or indicated themes, I have tried to fill the gap myself.

Since his preoccupations can be seen as emerging from his rather odd childhood, this first chapter gives an idea of the early forces at work on him. Further biographical material will be found in the discussion of the films which relate to episodes in his own life.

Truffaut's childhood was far from happy. His parents were somewhat eccentric and not particularly devoted to their child. As they both worked – his father as an architect and designer, his mother as a secretary – he was frequently left to his own devices. At weekends, they were inclined to set off for the mountains with rucksacks and not be seen again until Monday. The boy, left to run wild, became something of a delinquent. 'Mondays I would look at the social columns of the newspapers to see what my parents were doing . . . I was a child who huddled forgotten in the corner and dreamed . . . I still am.' He spent long periods of his childhood with his grandmother, and during the war was frequently packed off to 'holiday' camps. He was at one of these, where the director sold the boys' food on the black-market, when the Americans arrived to liberate the area. A little before their arrival he had escaped from the camp, an escape which was to form the basis of the final scene of *Les Quatre Cents Coups*. His 'home' was in the Clichy-Pigalle district, which has retained its strong emotional significance for him. He was never very attached to school and would frequently take days off to do the rounds of the local cinemas. His constant companion in these escapades was Robert Lachenay, who is transposed into René in *Les Quatre Cents Coups,* on which he was first assistant; he was also the stills photographer for

Tirez sur le pianiste. Speaking of Truffaut when he first knew him, towards the end of 1949, Jacques Rivette says ' . . . or suddenly, a photo revealed him three years before, at the fairground shooting range, a dazzled, pale, and smaller version of Robert Hossein, with alongside him, expansive Robert Lachenay . . .' The latter also gave his name to Pierre Lachenay, in *La Peau Douce*.

Truffaut's appetite for films was voracious and undiscriminating. It was during the final years of the war that he developed the total commitment to the cinema which led him to say that from then on there was never any other interest to rival it in his life, nor any other activity he would rather engage in.

Ironically, he came to films first through their dialogue, going to see those he loved best ten or a dozen times, until he knew the entire soundtrack off by heart. Films by Jean Renoir and those with dialogue by Jacques Prévert he could recite from beginning to end. From the age of twelve he kept a diary and listed in alphabetical order every film

From Borstal boy to music-lover: Antoine Doinel (Jean-Pierre Léaud) in Les Quatre Cent Coups *and* L'Amour a vingt ans.

*From courtship to marriage: Antoine Doinel
(Jean-Pierre Léaud) in* Baisers Volés *and* Domicile
Conjugal.

he saw, starring those he saw several times. Thus
he saw *La Règle du jeu* (Jean Renoir, 1939), *Le
Roman d'un tricheur* (Sacha Guitry, 1936), and
Le Corbeau (Henri-Georges Clouzot, 1943) at least
a dozen times each. When he enlisted in the army,
he had seen nearly two thousand films in six or
seven years, or as he puts it, 'I had lost at the
cinema some four thousand hours that I might
have devoted to literature.'

On leaving school at the age of fourteen, he took
a succession of jobs, as messenger boy, storeman,
office-worker, and later as a welder in a factory;
each of these he left or was asked to leave after a
matter of months. None of them interested him:
he lived solely for Sundays, when he could shut

Right: Jean Renoir in La Regle du jeu: *the most
important film-maker in the most important film.*

himself away in the cheaper suburban cinemas for the entire day. The cinema became the symbol of a finer and more intense existence, contrasting strongly with the grey deprivations of reality. 'I've always preferred transposed life to life itself. If at the age of eleven or twelve I already chose books and films, it was because I preferred to see life reflected through books and films . . . If I was asked what places I've most loved in my life, I'd say the countryside in Murnau's *Sunrise* or the city in the same film, but not a place I'd really visited, because I never really visit anything. I know it's a bit unusual, but I don't like landscapes or things. I like people; I'm interested in ideas and feelings.'

The opportunity to inhabit the outer fringes of this magical world was provided by the film society movement, then at the beginning of its immense post-war expansion. Not yet 16, he founded a ciné-club of his own in 1947 with what remained of his salary as a storeman. Its career was short-lived, but it provided the occasion for a meeting which was to transform his life: Truffaut's enterprise failed largely because it was in direct competition with the Ciné-club de la Chambre Noire, organised by André Bazin, whose acquaintance he made. Though only thirteen years older, Bazin came to take the place of a father to Truffaut.

As a result of bad administration, Truffaut found himself faced with mounting bills for which, as organiser, he was responsible. Before long a complaint was laid and he was arrested. Still barely more than a schoolboy, he found himself locked up with thieves and prostitutes (with whom he has since felt a sort of complicity), and then transported by police van to the Centre de Mineurs Délinquants, at Villejuif. André Bazin, no doubt fascinated by this boy whose passion for the cinema so resembled his own, managed to get him released from the Reform Centre on condition he visit a psychologist once a week – the inspiration for the interview with the psychologist in *Les Quatre Cents Coups*. From this point, Bazin was a sort of unofficial guardian to Truffaut, seeing a possible source of salvation for Truffaut in his passion for the cinema.

He introduced Truffaut to the group of enthusiasts who were setting up Objectif 49, which Jacques Doniol-Valcroze has said represented the first *prise de conscience* of the cinema by the post-war generation. It was a new type of ciné-club, presenting not classics of the cinema but new avant-garde films, often before their official release: it grouped together many prestigious directors and enthusiasts, among them Jean Cocteau, Robert Bresson, Roger Leenhardt, Alexandre Astruc, Pierre Kast and Raymond Queneau, as well as Doniol-Valcroze and Bazin. They were all to influence the growth of the concept, as yet not really developed or expressed, of a *cinéma d'auteurs*.

Towards the end of 1949, on visits to the Ciné-club du Quartier Latin, the Minotaure film bookshop, and the art cinemas, Truffaut met several others, his own age or a bit older, who were equally obsessed with the cinema. They included Jacques Rivette, then twenty, and Jean-Luc Godard, who was nineteen and theoretically taking courses at the Sorbonne. Godard was later to recall this period of their lives: 'It was a hot, heavy Saturday in July, I remember. We had left the Place Clichy . . . the most beautiful square in Paris, Truffaut was sure of that . . . we'd bought cigars next-door to the Atomic . . . then gone on to the Pax-Sèvres where my godmother had slipped us 10,000 francs, a month's advance . . . we went and saw *The Red Angel* with Tilda Tamar . . . "What a tremendous woman," François kept repeating . . . then we went on to the first session at the Avenue de Messine, where the disgusting Rossif took your tickets . . . Truffaut's great dream at that time was to live in the Hôtel Truffaut, rue Truffaut, but unfortunately the two weren't in the same suburb . . . this unique address that no postman will ever read . . . even in a novel by Giraudoux, whom he liked a little less than Balzac, and he's right . . . Truffaut, Paris . . . but he needn't worry . . . for hundreds of millions of spectators . . . in Chile, in Singapore, in Montreal, in Yokohama, in Helsinki . . . he sells well overseas . . . in short, a fairish number of men and women have read it written, like the watermark on high quality paper, in those faces – rather grave, romantic and touching faces – of Jules and the Pianist . . .'

In April 1950, Jean-Georges Auriol, who had founded and run La Revue du Cinéma, was killed in a motor accident. Doniol-Valcroze decided to continue his work and began setting up a new film magazine, based on Objectif 49, to replace La Revue du Cinéma, which had never been a commercial success. Meanwhile, Godard joined Doniol-Valcroze and Rivette in publishing critical pieces in a transitory broadsheet called La Gazette du Cinéma, in which their work appeared alongside that of Eric Rohmer. By Autumn 1950, plans for the new magazine had taken shape, and Les Editions de l'Etoile, the company which was to publish it, was founded in January 1951. The first number of Cahiers du Cinéma appeared on 1 April, 1951. The editors were still unpaid, and Bazin was already suffering from the illness which was finally to kill him in 1958; he only returned from convalescence in the Pyrenees to help with the second issue. During 1951, Cahiers published articles by all the Objectif 49 team, together with others by Rohmer, Rivette, Chris Marker, Paul Gégauff and Hans Lucas, as Godard preferred to sign himself.

But not by Truffaut. In 1951, he had volunteered for three years service in the armed forces, 'for personal reasons', as Antoine Doinel, his film equivalent, was later to explain. This proved to be a mistake. When his regiment was assigned to a tour of duty in Indo-China, Truffaut took advantage of a final leave to go AWOL. On the advice of Bazin, he gave himself up to the authorities, and was thrown into the military prison at the Dupleix barracks in Paris along with a crowd of deserters from the Korean war. In this establishment, amidst the smell of urine and with twelve crammed into a cell meant for four, Bazin and his wife Janine managed to contact Truffaut in August 1952 by pretending to be his parents. After six months of wrangling, they talked the authorities into demobilising him. The discharge, like Antoine's in Baisers Volés, was granted on the grounds of 'instability of character'. Once Truffaut was out of prison, Bazin got him a job with the Ministry of Agriculture's Centre Cinématographique, and introduced him to Cahiers, now well established and entering on its third year of publication. Reviews by Truffaut begin in Cahiers 21, March 1953, but his first major article was not published until Cahiers 31, January 1954. It was a landmark not only for Truffaut, but for the magazine itself.

In the brief history of Cahiers which he wrote for its hundredth issue, Doniol-Valcroze admits that until Truffaut's article, the group had lacked a unifying force, a common policy, a clear statement of values against which each new film could be measured. The article, *Une certaine tendance du cinéma français*, was a violent attack on the classic French cinema, with its 'tradition of quality', its teams of professionals specialising in their own small fields, its elaborately designed sets reconstructed in studios, and its unnatural, literary dialogue. Tracing the development of all this from the 'poetic realism' of the 'thirties, represented by Marcel Carné and Jacques Prévert, he defined a second post-war generation which aimed at 'psychological realism'. He blamed them for all the evils besetting the French cinema at that time. In particular, he was violently critical of such established figures as Claude Autant-Lara, Jean Delannoy, René Clément, Yves Allégret, plus the script-writers Henri Jeanson, Jean Aurenche, and Pierre Bost, who together formed the backbone of this cinema.

He dismissed the directors as faceless technicians, obediently and unimaginatively putting into images the detailed indications of the script-writers. The quality of their films depended primarily on the quality of the scenario. This in turn, since it probably came from Jeanson or Aurenche and Bost, was usually execrable. Not being cineastes themselves, the script-writers did not produce a potential film, but a work of literature which, perhaps admirable in itself, neither exploited nor even lent itself to the visual possibilities of the cinema. Moreover, under the guise of 'inventing equivalent scenes', they betrayed and perverted the famous books they specialised in adapting. On top of this, their principal fault was simply bad taste. 'I cannot see any possibility of peaceful coexistence between this "quality tradition" and a *"cinéma d'auteurs"*. It is the former which has turned the public against many of the masterpieces of the latter . . . To put an end to it, why don't we all . . . turn to adapting literary masterpieces, of which there are probably still a few left, and of course add a burial scene here and there? (A spiteful reference to *Jeux Interdits* directed by Clément in 1952 from an Aurenche and Bost script.) Then we'll all be in the "quality tradition" up to our necks, and the French cinema with its daring "psychological realism", its "harsh truths", its "rigour" and its "ambiguity" will be one great morbid funeral, ready to be heaved out of the Billancourt studios and stacked up in the cemetery so appropriately awaiting alongside . . .'

Such outspokenness was unknown in French critical circles, especially when directed at figures of such eminence. Doniol-Valcroze admits that he and Bazin had hesitated a long while before deciding to publish it. In the end, however, even if the judgments contained in it were often arbitrary and in individual cases unjust, the article justified itself: 'I do not seek to flatter Truffaut here, as he couldn't care less, nor to convince anyone that his articles are forever graven in marble. I simply note in all objectivity that the publication of this article marks the real point of departure of what, rightly, or wrongly, Cahiers du Cinéma signifies today (i.e. October 1959). A river had been crossed; a mechanism which was to carry us all along with it had been set in motion: we now had a common bond. From now on it was known we were for Renoir, Rossellini, Hitchcock, Cocteau, Bresson, and against X, Y and Z. From now on we had a doctrine, the *Politique des auteurs,* even if it lacked flexibility. The interviews with great directors were to follow naturally, and a real contact was to be established between them and us. Now our clan of Hitchcocko-Hawksians could be derided, our attacks on the "quality cinema" deprecated, the "young Turks" of criticism declared dangerous . . . An idea had been unleashed which was to proceed obstinately to its logical conclusion: the accession of almost all its supporters to the status of director.'

In the course of the next five years, Truffaut published about 75 articles, many of which are really manifestoes, some 25 interviews with favourite *auteurs* and reviews of several hundred films.

These appeared in Cahiers, in Cinémonde on which a friend had got him his first critical job writing imaginary biographies of American stars, in the transient right-wing magazine Temps de Paris from which he was sacked after a month for daring to criticise Michèle Morgan in a film by Jean Delannoy, and particularly in the literary weekly Arts. His famous Cahiers article had gained him entry here and he rapidly became its principal film critic, gathering around him a core of similarly-minded friends including Rivette, Rohmer, Charles Bitsch, Godard, Claude de Givray and Robert Lachenay. All his critical activity was based on the propositions contained in the original article, and aimed at transforming the existing cinema into a more personal means of expression in which he and his friends would eventually take part.

The basis of the *Politique des auteurs* had been drawn from Jean Renoir, who had some time previously proclaimed that 'the time of directors is over, and that of the author about to dawn: people will write their own scenarios, then go to the studios and realise their own conceptions.' Renoir's friend Giraudoux, had said something similar: 'There are no works, there are only authors.' Astruc and Cocteau had expressed these sentiments more recently, the former in his famous *Caméra-stylo* article in which he advocated using the camera as a writer uses his pen, and the latter in a revealing little phrase quoted by Truffaut: 'It's not what he does that makes an artist, it's what he *is*.' We see here the germs of the search underlying all Truffaut's films, the search for an intrinsic certainty and security, for essentially timeless values which allow one to distinguish the good from the bad, to separate once and for all the praiseworthy from the damnable. Throughout his critical career, he was to believe this possible, with the result that though he was often unjust, he was always forceful and effective in his criticism. Towards the end of his period as a critic, his faith in these absolute standards was to waver, and by the time he began making films the emphasis was on the infinitely subtle gradations between good and bad and the inextricable confusion of the comic and the tragic, with all categorical affirmations of absolute truths now relegated to the level of wistful regrets for a Paradise Lost.

In the meantime, however, his principles resulted in the condemnation of certain directors as irrevocably bad, while others were in his eyes fated to produce masterpieces, even if, as in the case of Jacques Becker's *Ali-Baba et les quarante voleurs,* several viewings and some verbal contortions were needed to reveal the master's hand. 'The productions signed Hunebelle, Lavison, Berthomieu, Lepage, Boyer, Chevalier, Lacombe, Decoin, Gaspard Huit, Kirsanoff, Gourguet, etc., not being any concern then for serious criticism, we will consider only such films as reveal a bare minimum of ambition.' 'In general, the French cinema, in its persistent mediocrity, has the advantage of offering with satisfying consistency the example of what is to be avoided at all costs.' 'Twenty years of adaptations which are criminal in their timidity have accustomed the public to a gilded insignificance.' Clouzot is accused of pandering to the public and of autocratic mishandling of actors.

After quoting Jeanson, he comments *'Il fait Kafka dans ses culottes'* – a play on the expression *'Il fait caca dans ses culottes'* said of small children who have been caught short. André Cayatte is described as 'a cheat and a lawyer, but not an artist.' On Carlo-Rim: 'What a quantity of vulgarity in one man: bad taste, ugliness, clumsiness, incompetence, facility and baseness of inspiration.' René Clair is 'official entertainer for elderly women'. René Clément 'manages to attain depths of vulgarity comparable to Autant-Lara'. With Autant-Lara himself he was engaged in a running battle over censorship, 'When I write that freedom of expression is total for a great cineaste, Claude Autant-Lara should not feel himself called into question, because he is not a great cineaste but rather a meticulous transposer of scenarios written by others. He is not a film-author, but an illustrator of texts . . . What he forgets to mention is that he *agrees* to bow to the censors' demands, not least because he gets his cut of the film's profits . . . Certainly censorship is a reality, since it suits his

book that it should be.' Autant-Lara was a natural enemy, being president of the film technicians' trade union and thus official figurehead and defender of the quality tradition, involving full use of studios and full employment of technicians. He was also the leading director of scripts by the reviled Aurenche and Bost.

Charles Spaak's scenarios, too, are 'full of pointless awkwardnesses, in their construction, scenarist's subterfuges, and aphorisms in dubious taste'. Clément's *Gervaise* is a film 'of profound futility', Luis Garcia Berlanga's *Calabuig* is idiotic and limping, its characters are not authentic, and in general 'the Spanish cinema does not exist'. The British cinema is even worse, and *ought* not to. Of Delbert Mann's *Desire under the Elms,* he says 'it's difficult to know what to detest most in this mechanical tragedy: the vileness of the settings, the ugliness of the photography, the grotesque acting, or the nullity of the direction'. About *L'Homme Traqué* he comments that 'there is no point in going to see this film, nor in putting much hope in the director's future'. As a final example, here is an extract from his review of Yves Allégret's *Méfiez-vous fillettes* (1957): 'This film is colourless, tasteless and of no particular odour; it's hard to see why it was banned, because it's no more vile than the bulk of the French production . . . Nothing which is insincere is of any significance, and *Méfiez-vous fillettes* is insincere. Yves Allégret has no more idea about writing scenarios than he has of directing; his work is void of all discrimination, taste, system, principle; he has nothing up his sleeves, nothing in his hands, nothing in his head. The scenario is not

Below left: La Jument Verte *of Claude Autant-Lara: too meticulous for Truffaut.*

good, but was rescuable if the job of adapting it had been given to anyone but René Wheeler, who generally fouls all he touches. [In Truffaut, the qualification 'generally' shows unusual generosity.] . . . Already, discussing the trivial cuts enforced by the Ministry, Georges Sadoul speaks of a "mutilated version". What a laugh. Can you mutilate a malignant tumour?'

Cited out of context, such examples could give the impression that Truffaut was irrationally castigating anything that conflicted with his prejudices. However, in general he was extremely specific and objective in giving the reasons for his judgments; once these judgments were formed, it became absolutely imperative that he should convince his readers of their validity and prevent them from patronising bad films.

His attacks were directed against the cinema's businessmen as well as some of its creators. The mild distaste that Truffaut had expressed at the 1956 Cannes Film Festival developed the next year into a splendidly insulting series of articles with a front-page headline announcing *Cannes: a flop characterised by compromises, underhand deals, and bungling.* It was a mere publicity performance designed to fill the hotels in the off-season. The festival was ruled by money: for the film world its sole significance was as a market where contracts and co-productions were finalised. Nowhere was there any interest in art, or artistic integrity. Further, he attacked the one-film-per-country system, which resulted in official, 'acceptable' selections on grounds of their propaganda value to their countries. He attacked the exceptions to the system, which permitted the USA and the USSR to use political and economic pressure and get several films each shown at the best times. The chief administrator, Robert Favre Le Bret, was picked out for individual vilification. The jury were 'a pack of incompetents who doze through the first afternoon session (their siesta hour) and who, to "help formulate their ideas", each morning snatch up the reviews in Le Figaro, telephoned in, alas, by the dopiest of my colleagues, Louis Chauvet himself, the Delannoy of the short-sighted ball-point.' ('*Le Delannoy de la pointe bic à courte vue*' – a play on the title of Agnès Varda's *La Pointe*

Courte which Chauvet had derided.) He was the only important French film critic not invited the next year, 1958. This did not stop him repeating his accusations, though less virulently, for reforms were at last taking place; ironically, his own film was to be selected in 1959, and awarded the prize for direction.

On other fronts he attacked the distributors, who had no idea what the public wanted, he attacked the government, for misuse of subsidies, and he attacked the archaic laws controlling the industry. He even attacked the quality of film publicity and trailers, but most treacherously of all, he attacked the ignorance of his fellow-critics. He went so far as to divide them into seven categories – those ignorant of film history, those ignorant of cinematic techniques, the chauvinist, the insolent and the professorial, those living in the past, and those simply lacking in all imagination. In each relevant category he listed by name the more famous critics, excepting only Bazin, the sole critic of intelligence and integrity.

The result was four years of vicious in-fighting in the film world, and the reluctant growth in France of a climate of self-criticism for which Truffaut is largely to be thanked. Certainly no one thought of doing so at the time. The most hated man in professional film circles, he was variously described by colleagues as 'chief scandal-maker of Arts', 'cruellest of contemporary critics' and 'the most virulent, talented and detested critic of his generation', whose articles have 'dynamited the foundations of the old cinema'. The industry named him and Bazin as the prime enemies of the cinema as a popular amusement. There were even personal threats from individuals he had publicly mocked. Because of a sarcastic review of his first film, Robert Hossein threatened to punch Truffaut in the face next time he saw him. In the course of a similar review of his second film, Truffaut ruefully admitted that 'this encounter has not yet taken place, and I don't know whether to be glad about that or not. If he had carried out his threat with the barest minimum of success, Robert Hossein would have earned for himself amongst the members of his profession something of the admiration and fellow-feeling that his film could never arouse.'

But if Truffaut was so violent in his campaigning, the violence derived solely from his total commitment to the cinema, which he has expressed most movingly, many times. Normally, he is quite the opposite of a violent man. Doniol-Valcroze, pointing out the genial charm which pervades *Tirez sur le pianiste,* wrote 'It's all rather ironic when you consider the reputation François Truffaut carved out for himself . . . ironic, but not absurd, for it's not surprising that this timid and yet exacting love for the cinema should have been mistaken for viciousness and aggressiveness'. As Charlie said to Clarisse in that film, 'haven't you heard of the recklessness of timid people?' Outraged that this great art form was being perverted at the hands of people *who didn't love the cinema* (Truffaut's own italics, expressing incredulity), this mild man found the courage to speak out.

At first his intention was simply to reform, but he became progressively more convinced that it would be necessary first to destroy the rotting hulk of the traditional cinema before attempting to build something more worthwhile. 'When things aren't going too well in the cinema, our only hope must be that the columns of the temple, slowly transformed into a brothel, will crumble, encouraging a renewal from the base up . . . The moment has come, for the edifice is tottering.'

Reading his admiring and often perceptive reviews of films by the directors he already considered *auteurs* – among the French, Renoir, Abel Gance, Cocteau, Bresson, Jacques Tati, and later Roger Leenhardt and Jacques Becker – one can predict the qualities he will aim at in his own work, which like that of these directors is the direct and consistent expression of a single personality. 'I don't believe in good and bad films; I believe in good and bad directors . . . Essentially, a gifted and intelligent director remains gifted and intelligent whatever the film he's making. So I'm in favour of judging, when it's a question of judging, not films but directors. I will never like a film made by Delannoy. I will always like a film made by Renoir . . . It seems to me that tomorrow's film will be even more personal than a novel, more

individual and autobiographical than a confession or a private diary. Young cineastes will express themselves in the first person, and talk about things that have happened to them; perhaps an account of their first love or their most recent, the growth of their political awareness, or a travel tale, an illness, their military service, their marriage, their last holidays; and these will automatically please, because they'll be true and fresh . . . Tomorrow's film will not be made by employees going about their daily routine, but by artists for whom the shooting of a film constitutes an exciting and exalting adventure. Tomorrow's film will resemble the man who makes it, and the number of spectators will be proportional to the number of friends of the director. Tomorrow's film will be an act of love.'

His reviews already show a preoccupation with 'realism': he praises the wide screen less for attracting people away from their television screens than for allowing the creation of a wider context around the characters, approximating to our vision of the real world; he likes colour film less for its expressive potential than for representing a further step towards realism. He sees films as bad when they conform to stereotypes or categories and good when they are inconsistent in tone, blend genres and mix emotions, when they show characters in whom conflicting good and bad impulses produce apparently contradictory and illogical actions. He admires Renoir for 'the bitterness of the gay moments, the clownishness of the sad', and Bergman because 'from devotion to truth, he develops his work in all different directions at once'.

During his years as a critic he saw several directors attempting to develop along similar lines, among them Astruc, Louis Malle, Georges Franju, Alain Resnais and Agnès Varda. He praised Roger Vadim's first two films for authentically recreating the sensation of being young and in love, but yet not falling back on the sentimental clichés of poetic realism. He appreciated the 'personal notations', the direct or indirect indications of tastes in cinema, literature or anything else; as well as providing an added richness for the enthusiasts, these also help impose the consistent stamp of a single personality on all a director's films.

However, more such directors were needed: the Cahiers group had yet to begin its first professional films. The formulae for this evolution were frequently proclaimed by Truffaut. The principal problem was so to reduce the cost of these early attempts that anyone at all, without technical competence or commercial backing, could express himself as readily in this art-form as in any other. 'Anyone can be a director, anyone can be a script-writer, anyone can be an actor; it's only the job of the cameraman that requires some rudimentary training. . . . [If you go into the cost,] you come to the stunning conclusion that, in a country where the average cost of a film oscillates around 90 million francs, a guy with something to get off his chest, as they say, can make a film for four or five million francs.'

To achieve this, he advocated quitting the studios to make films in natural settings. Not only was this cheaper but it looked more authentic: the French cinema had too long depended on painted trees seen through painted windows. Secondly, it was wrong to prefer star performers, because they cost too much and are capable only of stereotyped roles. Being more preoccupied with their own image than with the final product, stars can exercise undue control over a film. Truffaut believed in total freedom to use anyone who happened to correspond to the physical and mental characteristics of a particular role, wherever he was found. Agreeing with Renoir that an actor only revealed himself, or rather was revealed to himself, in the course of a film, Truffaut argued that the director should aim, not to get a 'good actor', but to choose the *right* actor, the one in whom he has foreseen the ability to grow into the role.

Finally, with the crew much reduced and composed mostly of friends working for love, to be paid only if the film made a profit, it should be possible to reduce shooting time to a few weeks and the costs to the bare price of the film stock and camera hire. By avoiding the sort of literary scripts which in the past have resulted in a form of filmed theatre, with the camera reduced to film-ing the tableaux imagined by the writer, the cinema of the future would be free to use more agile camera movement which would follow the actors and action freely. Summarising the changes he hoped to see introduced by the younger directors, Truffaut said: 'They must film different things, in a different spirit. They must desert the studios, which are too costly (and are anyway merely shacks, noisy, insalubrious, and badly equipped) to invade the sunny beaches where no cineaste (save Vadim) has dared set up his camera. The sun costs less than lighting and generators. They must film in the streets, and even in real apartments . . . If a young director wants to film a love scene, instead of having his actors mouth the stupid dialogue by Charles Spaak, he should call to mind the conversation he had the night before with his wife, or – why not – let the actors find for themselves the words they're accustomed to saying . . . The young cineaste must work neither against the producer, nor against the public, but rather convince them, devastate them, seduce them, win them over to his way of thinking. He must be madly ambitious and madly sincere.'

It is well known that the New Wave developed along much the same lines as Truffaut prescribed. What is less known is that, of all those who were to form the group, he alone had clearly and concisely enunciated these principles over the preceding years. Jean-Luc Godard, for instance, may have shared them, but his articles are incoherent in their expression and vague and emotive in allotting praise and blame; they add up to no consistent plan of action. Bazin's writing was more intellectual and theoretical than his disciple's: he could never have expressed so forcefully the general principles which he undoubtedly contributed to formulating because from the start he was scrupulously aware of the infinite qualifications which were necessary to a just appreciation even of a bad film. Truffaut was never predominantly concerned with justice, but was motivated by indignation at the compromises and concessions made by so many people unworthy of the art they professed. Only Truffaut, engaged in his cinematic Holy War, managed to combine simplicity of expression with sufficient passion to render his articles comprehensible and effective. Towards the end, and with final victory in sight, Truffaut's articles begin to acquire something of Bazin's more balanced approach, something of the awareness of gradations and complexities which he already admired in the films of others and which was to characterise his own. Though still tending wholly to praise or wholly to condemn a film, he began to find himself supporting some which his principles should logically have led him to condemn. One can feel a certain embarrassment at such moments. He even found himself praising Autant-Lara's *La Traversée de Paris* (1956) and *En cas de malheur* (1958), despite the fact that 'a few years ago, with all the purity of my twenty years, I would have condemned such a film *in toto,* and it's with a certain bitterness that I catch myself today admiring a film more intelligent than beautiful, more clever than noble, more cunning than sensitive.'

As relief from these constant verbal battles, and 'to keep himself sane', Truffaut, with his friends, had been experimenting with cameras and preparing ideas for their future films. From the original scenario of *Les Quatre Cents Coups,* it seems quite possible that it was written as early as 1950, when Truffaut was eighteen. This and the scenario of *Les Mistons* were only two of a whole series of outlines by Truffaut on the theme of childhood. In 1955 or 1956, he also developed the original version of *A bout de souffle,* which he conceived more or less as a sequel to *Les Quatre Cents Coups* – what Antoine might be like four years later, after several reform schools and military service. Edouard Molinaro read it, and wanted to use it for his first feature; when his producers refused it, he went on to make *Le Dos au mur.* Truffaut twice attempted to shoot it

Belmondo in A Bout de souffle: *Antoine Doinel four years on, but* à la *Godard.*

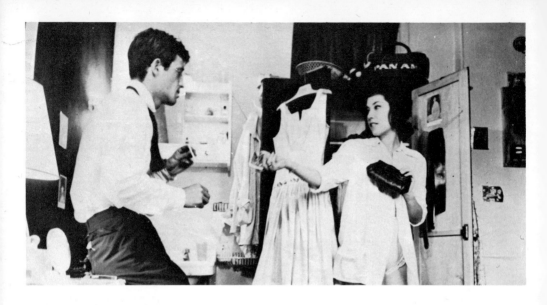

A Bout de souffle: *Belmondo nowhere near getting married.*

himself, the first time with Jean-Claude Brialy, the second with Gérard Blain, but each time circumstances prevented him. Subsequently, he forgot all about it, until reminded by Godard, who went on (after Truffaut had made *Les Mistons* and *Les Quatre Cents Coups*) to use it so successfully for his own first feature that it has come to be identified with him. When Truffaut handed it to Godard, it consisted of fifteen typed pages (since reprinted in L'Avant-Scène du Cinéma 79), and though Godard transformed it into something personal, it's still remarkable how many of the qualities often attributed to Godard were already present in the original. Like *Tirez sur le pianiste*, it is a pastiche of the American gangster film, but the casual quality, so foreign to the gangster films but so typical of Truffaut, is already there. So is the common reverence of both men for the cinema, which appears in the many personal notations,

such as the Humphrey Bogart gestures and the visits to the movies whenever there's a gap in the action.

But in 1955, the possibility of realising any of these scenarios still seemed remote; on the other hand, for critics in close contact with all branches of the industry, the possibility of borrowing a 16 mm camera was much more real. The group admired Molinaro for having managed to find a commercial outlet for his 16 mm production; they knew that Astruc's mastery at the start of his directorial career was due to practice in this format, though he steadfastly refused to let anyone see his 16 mm efforts. Within the group, Eric Rohmer had already made two shorts, and had begun a full-length film based on one of the Comtesse de Ségur's tales, though never finishing it. Jacques Rivette had arrived in Paris, some years before, with an experimental 16 mm short in his suitcase; since then he had made two more. As practice, he agreed to help with Truffaut's first attempt by doing the camera-work. This was Truffaut's only amateur film. It was in Doniol-

Valcroze's apartment, with Doniol-Valcroze's daughter as the central character.

The other three actors were also children. Feeling he would be overawed at having to direct adults, he wanted to begin with actors he could control completely. Besides, he was still only about 22, and most of his ideas for films related to childhood situations. He began work with no scenario at all, and only vague ideas of what he wanted to achieve. Practically the whole film was improvised on the spot, which he admits was fatal, especially for an amateur film. Of this early experiment, generally referred to under the title *Une Visite,* he has said that the most instructive part was the attempt to construct a coherent film out of his random scraps of material. He found he had no sense of ellipsis, with the result that half of each day's film consisted of people opening and shutting doors, and had to be rejected. However, he borrowed some editing equipment and, with the help of Alain Resnais, tried to impose some form on it. It still ended up 'incomprehensible and unprojectable', 'of no interest to anyone, even at the time'. It was two years before he tried again and produced something more acceptable: *Les Mistons.*

Meanwhile, he would have felt honoured to watch some of his favourite directors at work, despite his frequent assertions that no formal training was necessary (or as Chabrol put it: 'All you need to know to direct a film can be learned in four hours. The courses at IDHEC instead of lasting two years, should last half a day.') Truffaut managed to get a contract as second assistant to Max Ophüls, who was beginning what was to prove his last film, *Lola Montès.* Unfortunately, after a disagreement with the director of production, he ripped up the contract – an action he has regretted ever since. During 1956 and 1957 he had a job as assistant to Rossellini, with whom

New wave aristocracy: Jean-Pierre Léaud, Jean-Claude Brialy, François Truffaut and Jeanne Moreau.

he worked on three scenarios which were never used.

During 1956, Vadim's success with *Et Dieu Cré la femme*, and Agnès Varda's achievement in realising the ambitious *La Pointe Courte* for twelve million francs, led Truffaut and his friends to formulate a scheme which would permit several of them to make their first films: since the average cost of a film was little under 100 million francs, and they were convinced they could produce them for as little as 20 million, they would offer a producer five films for the price of one. And so that the producer would not take fright at the thought of so many untried directors, they would get the help of Astruc and Resnais. Thus, Resnais, for instance, would shoot the first one with Rivette as assistant (it was to be *Les Mauvais Coups*, adapted from Roger Vailland's novel), Astruc would shoot the second with Truffaut as assistant, Rivette the third and Truffaut the fourth, with other members of the group as assistants, and so on. The system never came to anything, largely because producers were simply not interested in making cheap films.

The one concrete result of this collaboration was a script, *Les Quatre Jeudis*, written by four of these Cinéastes Associés – Truffaut, Rivette, Chabrol and Charles Bitsch. It ran to some five hundred pages, and was built around a central figure to be played by Jean-Claude Brialy, of all the friends the most surely destined for an acting career. According to Truffaut, the script must be lying in every drawer, every cellar and every attic of every director. Not one, however, showed any interest.

Impatient with all the delays, Rivette, who (ironically, in view of the way things turned out) was by far the most convinced of his vocation as a director, set about preparing a smaller-scale work within their own financial and technical reach; it became *Le Coup du berger*. He developed the story from a news item heard over the radio. Chabrol wrote the dialogue and set about financing it (reputedly by not buying any records for three months). The film stock was the only real cost, as the camera was loaned free in exchange for an advertisement in the back of Cahiers.

The producer Pierre Braunberger, who financed so many experiments around this time, saw it, put up the money for the soundtrack and distributed it both to film societies and through normal commercial channels. It eventually appeared in the cinemas at precisely the same time as Truffaut's *Les Mistons,* in which the lovers are seen watching a short section of it. According to Truffaut *Le Coup du berger* was the principal incentive and starting point for all the Cahiers team in their film-making efforts. It had cost $1\frac{1}{2}$ million francs all told, which made it apparent that their calculations of 20 million for a feature film were realistic. Godard and Rohmer became more ambitious in their Charlotte series, Chabrol prepared to start work on *Le Beau Serge* (which he had previously offered to Rossellini), and Truffaut organised three of his own scenarios based on childhood into a series of 20-minute sketches. His intention was to film the autobiographical one first, but towards the middle of 1957, Gérard Blain, whom he intended to use in the second one, announced that he was free. Consequently, Truffaut decided to defer *Les Quatre Cents Coups* and begin work straight away on his adaptation of *Les Mistons*. (The title translates roughly as 'brats', or simply 'kids', and is a southern equivalent of gosses. From *nid* – nest – comes *nistoun* – nestling or youngster – and the local variant of this in Nîmes, where the film was shot, is *mistoun or miston*.)

It might seem strange that Truffaut should have chosen an adaptation for his first film, that he should have preserved much of its literary style, and that he should have chosen a setting so remote from his own childhood experience. In retrospect, however, the short story he adapted can be seen to treat many of the themes around which his later films were to be built. In rudimentary form, his 'cult of friendship' is already present in this band of young boys. Children, particularly children on the verge of adolescence, are present in nearly all his films. The boys in *Les Mistons* experiencing the first glimmerings of sexuality anticipate Antoine's exaggerated consciousness of his mother's legs in *Les Quatre Cents Coups*. Most notably, Bernadette, the object of their fascination, who both attracts and terrifies them, starts the series of romanticised visions of womanhood that disturb the lives of all Truffaut's male protagonists. None of his men will be any more capable of coping with the incarnations of their ideals than are these young boys.

The film was an opportunity to experiment with various techniques, and the most successful are those devoted to the evocation of an atmosphere of awed reverence. The 'stopped images' when the boy stoops to smell Bernadette's bicycle seat are unexpectedly effective in suggesting a sort of religious ritual. Their later use to recall the lovers' final kiss, which is in such stark contrast with the more sordid surrounding images of adolescence, combines this awed reverence with the unreality of scenes remembered. Something of the same effect is achieved more simply in the scene in which one of the boys rushes to fetch the ball for Bernadette, and in a suddenly slow and ritual motion returns it to her, momentarily a communicant in a strange religion.

But not all the effects used in the film are so demonstrably related to the themes: many are simply the self-conscious visual balancing of masses and patterns of light and shade by a director determined to replace ugly studio-made films with a cinema exploiting the potential of natural settings. The compositions can seem forced and gratuitous. The lovers pause unnaturally against photogenic backgrounds; we see them framed by the bars of an iron gate and outlined against the sky at the top of the Nîmes arena. The intercut shots of the lovers in the arena are so awkward that one can't help imagining the camera having to leap instantaneously between the heights of the arena wall and the sandy floor. Equally unsuccessful is a shot of one bicycle lying on top of the other following a shot of their owners in the same position.

Even more gratuitous are the innumerable cross references to other films which occur throughout *Les Mistons*, the personal notations, which sometimes dominate the plot and become the principal centre of interest. After seeing *Le Coup du berger*, the boys tear up a poster for Jean Delannoy's *Chiens Perdus sans collier*, chanting 'Colliers *perdus sans chien*' – among Delannoy's films, Truffaut had particularly hated this one, because it hadn't attempted to capture the reality of childhood. There is an accurate re-creation of one of the moments in the first Lumière programme, screened at the end of 1895: a man is hosing the grass near the tennis court; the boys step on the hose, he peers into it, and the water spurts out into his face. This allusion to the cinema's first gag was included primarily as homage from a beginner to the original beginner, but also to show that such visual gags have lost none of their impact over the intervening sixty years. The scene is even given the jerky flickering motion associated with early films. A similar spirit inspired the reverse-motion 'resurrection' of the machine-gunned child.

There is a reference to Luis Buñuel's *Archibaldo de la Cruz* in the scene in which a passer-by refuses Gérard a light. The whole atmosphere of the film seems to be an attempt to recapture the airy, sunlit feeling of Renoir's *Partie de campagne,* and Jean Vigo's *Zéro de conduite* creeps into the lovers' conversation on the grass, when they associate the title with that other phrase so often used in Vigo's film *'consigné dimanche'*. Vigo's film was, of course, a more profound influence on *Les Quatre Cents Coups*, representing for Truffaut the exact opposite of the Delannoy opus, a genuine evocation of childhood.

What might seem surprising in a director so conscious of the visual potential of his medium is the use of a commentary overlaying the images in all his films until *La Peau Douce*. There are, however, precedents in such films by Cahiers favourites as Jean-Pierre Melville's *Le Silence de la mer* and *Bob le flambeur* and Robert Bresson's *Le Journal d'un curé de campagne* and *Un Condamné à mort s'est échappé*. (In Melville's films, too, can be found an antecedent for New Wave shooting methods and for tiny crews; his important early films were shot by Henri Decaë, who was to photograph *Les Quatre Cents Coups* and Chabrol's first four features.) It is noticeable that these commentaries become increasingly cool and understated, until finally in *Jules et Jim* (and later in *L'Enfant Sauvage*) they are used to tone

François Truffaut as D. W. Griffith.

down the images they accompany. In *Les Mistons,* however, the commentary is extremely literary – it was written by the author of the original story. Inevitably it detracts from the immediacy and reality which Truffaut was intent on achieving, and achieved so well in *Les Quatre Cents Coups.*

The shooting of *Les Mistons* began on 5 August 1957, and despite an interruption of ten days was completed a month later. Truffaut explains that he began rather hesitantly because he was extremely nervous. This was the crucial moment when he would discover whether he had been justified in all his dogmatic statements over the preceding years: here he was with no training, and a cast composed of children, one little-known actor who happened to be his friend, and that friend's wife, attempting to make a film for commercial release. 'I had enormous doubts: what if I was wrong, and the defenders of traditional methods correct?' He had little money, and because he was working outside the traditional system, he had no guarantee of distribution. To make the enterprise sound more official, he formed a production company, called Les Films du Carrosse in homage to Renoir's *Le Carrosse d'or* (1952), and conferred the title of Director of Production on his friend Robert Lachenay.

His timidity led him to shoot the film in a curious order: wanting to avoid being seen while making his first attempts, he started with the scenes in the empty arena at Nîmes, with only close friends involved. When he began working with the children, his doubts increased, not least because their attitude brought home to him the artificiality of the premise on which the film is based: they were carefree and spontaneous, slightly incredulous of the idea of spying on the loving couple, and much more interested in playing amongst themselves. Though mildly appreciative of Bernadette, they couldn't bring themselves to believe in the jealousy they were called on to act. 'It was at that moment I decided that if ever I used children again, it would only be in a film that meant something real to them.'

After the sad results of his earlier attempts at improvisation, Truffaut kept fairly close to the written scenario. About two-thirds of the film as we see it now is identical with the script, and the original version was even closer. Truffaut has always considered his films as subject to constant revision, and at various stages considerable portions of *Les Mistons* have been deleted. Reviewing an early public screening, Georges Sadoul could already say that the first version he had seen was somewhat verbose and diffuse, but that now 'the editing has been tightened up and silences put where they were needed'. Truffaut became more and more dissatisfied with the inflated literary and poetic sections; when he reworked the film into its present form for reissue with *Les Quatre Cents Coups* in 1967, he severely shortened the commentary and cut several of the lyrical dialogues between the lovers. The directions said 'They are manifestly crazy with joy at being together: chaste, and anxious to avoid all salaciousness,

22

they "act out" their feelings, and this acting – spontaneously invented as they go along – is full of strange changes in tone, with moments of truth breaking in here and there.' All this has disappeared, and the film is the better for it. The weight of the film is thus shifted towards the children, who are presented more sympathetically than in the original. Much of their sexual education, suggested in quick flashes towards the end, has been cut, so that the film may seem to end rather abruptly now, a small price to pay for the elimination of some embarrassing moments.

Given all Truffaut's doubts and hesitations, it came as something of a surprise to him to find that the finished product was projectable. Aside from private screenings for friends, the film seems to have had its first public showings *hors concours* at the Tours festival of short films in late 1957, and again *hors concours* (like *Le Beau Serge*) at the Cannes festival in May 1958. When the film reached the cinemas in November 1958, it was well received. Some critics went so far as to announce that a great director had been born, but they were mostly friends and colleagues. Even Truffaut's many enemies showed a considerable respect for the film, though few could resist contrasting the lyricism of the film with the vitriol that had flowed from his pen.

'Single-mindedness had paid off: at twenty-seven I had already been waiting fifteen years for this moment. I decided to be a director at the age of twelve. All my efforts since that time had been directed towards this one end. So it was natural that one day I should achieve it.' Yet even at the time he realised that *Les Mistons* was a step in the wrong direction; he was so little satisfied with it that what was to have been part of a triptych remained an isolated experiment. Subsequently his judgment was to become even harsher, until he came to see it as his least successful film. 'Objectively, I think one must go back to basic intentions to like it. The execution leaves a lot to be desired: the actors and dialogue are awful, and the whole thing is prodigiously formless and gauche . . . You can perhaps see what I was trying to do, and that's why people are indulgent. I feel like withdrawing it from circulation when I re-see it, yet there are good things: Bernadette Lafont and the feeling of sun . . . but you need a lot of indulgence really to like it.'

In 1958, the spring rains caused extensive flooding around Paris. Truffaut went to Pierre Braunberger to ask for film to elaborate an idea he had in mind. Jean-Claude Brialy agreed to act in it; Chabrol loaned his car. But by the time they reached the floods, the water had largely disappeared. The little that was left didn't inspire them, and anyway, amidst people trying desperately to save a few of their belongings it seemed almost indecent to rent a boat and start acting. Still, they went ahead, and Truffaut had to inform Pierre Braunberger that they had managed to waste all 600 metres of film. Then Godard said that perhaps he could salvage something, edited together the fragments and added a commentary. Even so, the result was hardly impressive. Truffaut said of it: 'I think you'll agree that it's neither Godard's best film nor Truffaut's best film . . . Obviously, once the thing was finished, it didn't really belong to either of us. The only logical thing to do was to sign it jointly and make a present of it to the producer, who didn't make any great fortune out of it.' It was given the title *Une Histoire d'eau*, probably by Godard, from Pauline Réage's novel, 'Histoire d'O' (Olympia Press).

It begins with a woman setting out from the outskirts of Paris to make her way to the University across rain-flooded country side. She is given a lift by Jean-Claude Brialy, but they are repeatedly thwarted, diverted, bogged down and even cast adrift in a boat, only to end up back at their car. The characters come to share the waywardness of the narrative, and the woman, content to spend most of the day straying back and forth across flooded fields, frequently seems to forget the original purpose of her journey. Her meandering route is echoed in the constant digressions which, far from being side-tracks, become the whole point of the film. Aragon is quoted as having begun a lecture on Plutarch with three-quarters of an hour of irrelevancies, and when a student wanted him to get back to the subject, calmly concluded his sentence: '. . .

Truffaut with Claude Jade and Jean-Pierre Léaud on the set of Domicile Conjugal.

for the whole art of Plutarch is in his digressions.' The film looks forward to *A bout de souffle* and to *Tirez sur le pianiste,* in that a comparatively insignificant story is used as a vehicle for personal meditations which are the real point of the film. It is also reminiscent of one of Truffaut's first reviews in which, having spent fifty lines discussing anything but the film, he ends up 'You'll tell me I've scarcely covered my subject. This is precisely what I hold against the director of *Snows of Kilimanjaro*.'

The commentary which overlays the film is once again literary to the point of intoxication. There is a deliberate discrepancy between image and text: they rarely correspond exactly, but follow their own wilful courses in an amusing counterpoint, meeting at odd moments and parting again. Dedicated to 'Mac Sennett', the film is packed

with references to the two men's favourite authors. As well as Aragon, often quoted by Godard, and Paul Eluard whom we meet again in *Pierrot le fou,* we are introduced to Truffaut's two favourite writers, Balzac and Giraudoux, as well as Raymond Chandler, Baudelaire, Valéry, Larbaud and perhaps others. The only cineaste who definitely achieves this same distinction is Georges Franju, whose early shorts they had both greatly admired.

The film was not distributed by Pierre Braunberger until March 1961, when it was used with Godard's final short *Charlotte et son Jules* as the supporting programme for Jacques Demy's *Lola.* By that time, of course, the New Wave was well and truly established, and the two shorts were treated as little more than an interesting sidelight on the earlier years of the two directors. One critic called *Une Histoire d'eau* 'a modest attempt by two cineastes to stir up some muddy water in the evident intention of creating a Wave'.

Les Quatre Cents Coups

Truffaut had intended to make this film before *Les Mistons*, but had deferred it because Gérard Blain was available for the latter. It was originally conceived as a companion piece to *Les Mistons*, a short sketch lasting about 20 minutes and entitled *La Fugue d'Antoine*. However, with *Les Mistons* finished, he had no money to proceed with any other shorts, and he realised that his projects for shorts included two distinct types of film: the first literary, the second either autobiographical or drawn from accounts of incidents that had actually happened. He felt that the two didn't mix.

La Fugue d'Antoine was autobiographical. It told the story of a boy at school who lies to explain being absent and, afraid to return home for fear of being found out, spends the night on the streets of Paris. This became transformed little by little into 'a sort of chronicle of the age of thirteen which I found the most interesting, while unfortunately it lost an aspect that meant a lot to me: Paris during the Occupation, the problems of the Black Market, and so on. Cinematic recreation of this was impossible for me, both financially and aesthetically, because in trying to evoke this period it is much too easy to make a fool of yourself.' Speaking in 1970, he said that he intended to fill this gap in his autobiography. When making *Les Quatre Cents Coups* he hadn't dared to try to recreate the Occupation, 'but in fact, my life at Antoine's age was tightly bound up with alarm sirens at night, air-raid shelters, and getting enough food. So I still have the feeling I should make a film on the Occupation, though without the Resistance.' Of the seven or eight scenarios he had to hand, his personal preference was for *La Fugue*

d'Antoine and he decided to go ahead with it.

Because he was disappointed with *Les Mistons,* he abandoned the idea of a film made of a series of such sketches in favour of turning this one story into a feature. As the scenario grew in length, he felt the need for a professional script-writer to sketch in the dialogue, to give some order to his ideas and to bring an element of objectivity into material that was all too personal. He had liked Marcel Moussy's book 'Sang Chaud' and his dialogue for the television show 'Si c'était vous'. He therefore provided Moussy with thumbnail sketches of the four principal characters and was delighted with the results of his work: 'Myself, I would have tended to type the parents, rather along the lines of a caricature, producing a non-objective satire. Moussy helped me to make them more human, more normal . . . I saw straight away that it was impossible to write dialogue for the children; we gave them the situations and they themselves provided the phrases. On the other hand, Moussy wrote all the dialogue for the parents, the teacher, etc., precisely as they are heard – he was a teacher himself for a while and used his own experience for the school scenes. He also helped me to give a structure to the scenario. I had pages and pages of notes, but it was all so close to me that I couldn't manage to put them into shape.'

After his experience with *Les Mistons,* he was a bit nervous about working with children again: he swore that he would never use as many as five in one film. In *Les Quatre Cents Coups,* however, he ended up with over a hundred. During the shooting, he repeated his resolve never to use chil-

Les Quatre Cent Coups: *Antoine Doinel (Jean-Pierre Léaud) in the hands of P'tite Feuille (Guy Decomble).*

dren again, but as he has said, 'Making films with children is a great temptation before, something of a panic during, but a great satisfaction after. Even when everything seems to be coming adrift, there's always something worth saving, and the child is always the best thing on the screen . . . A child's truth is something I think I feel absolutely. For example, throughout the film I had to struggle against Jean-Pierre Léaud. He was terrified people weren't going to like him. He was always wanting to smile. For three months I was

continually stopping him from smiling . . . And I'm sure I was right.'

Such confidence is rare in Truffaut. His uncertainty can be seen in the frequent use of children in his early films. He often felt intimidated by adult actors' experience: unsure of his own ideas, he was too ready to let them impose theirs. In any case, using children was almost inevitable if Truffaut wished to abide by his principles of authenticity: Truffaut's experience related largely to childhood and adolescence. Further, he felt that this subject, so real to him, had been inadequately treated by the cinema, mainly because of the star system. There were few, if any, fourteen-year-old stars. Where children appeared, they tended either to get shouldered aside to make room for the adult stars (like Gabin in *Chiens Perdus sans collier*) or made to act like miniature adults (as in *Jeux Interdits*); alternatively, actors already in their twenties play the children's parts. In all these cases the children's world is grossly distorted. Worse still, films frequently try to poeticise childhood, to surround it with a rosy glow. This, he says, results in films about red balloons, about white horses with flowing manes, but not about children. He was afraid that he had fallen into this trap in *Les Mistons*. In *Les Quatre Cents Coups*, he hoped to avoid it, but feels now that he still wasn't always strict enough with himself. He had been delighted by the children's reactions to the Punch and Judy show, which he filmed with a hidden camera, but had managed to prune half an hour of film down to thirty seconds or so. However, there is still the scene where the children, having stolen the typewriter, pass some pigeons which take fright and fly off. It's pretty, but pointless. He excuses himself on the grounds that at least he's aware of the sentimentality; it's a brief scene and anyway was a triumph for Henri Decaë, who had filmed it right on the Champs Elysées without anyone noticing him.

Finding the children proved easy: a friend put an advertisement in France Soir, which brought in over 200 applicants. Eliminating the provincial applicants, he gave 16 mm trials to the rest. Jean-Pierre Léaud stood out immediately. He had already played a small part in Georges Lampin's *La Tour prend garde* two years before and done a bit of post-synchronisation. His parents were both connected with the cinema; his mother was an actress, Jacqueline Pierreux, and his father an assistant director. But also, he had suffered rather similar trials to Truffaut himself, as his parents (who were present at the Cannes première) were only too willing to admit. There were other children Truffaut could have chosen who resembled him more: 'less aggressive, more shy, more

Les Quatre Cent Coups: *Antoine takes the rubbish out in filial piety.*

introverted', but their acting range would not have been as wide as Léaud's. However, a lot of scenes had to be cut from the existing scenario simply because they were too weak for Léaud's personality.

Money was still a problem. However much he reduced the costs, Truffaut would still have to pay out some 25 million francs. This was covered partly by the *prime à la qualité* accorded to *Les Mistons*. The rest he managed to borrow from his friends and his father-in-law.

But it was still necessary to economise. The adult roles were allotted to comparatively little-known actors, who were paid on a 'deferred shares' system, by which a proportion of their wages came out of profits, if any. The technical team was kept to a minimum – not a 'working minimum', as in Chabrol's first film, but a 'legal minimum', keeping to the regulations laid down by the trades unions. There was therefore no need for special permission before the film could be distributed, as there was with *Le Beau Serge*. But like Chabrol, he totally avoided the use of studios. These economies amounted to a 40% saving on costs. In view of the autobiographical element, he shot the film in areas of Paris he knew well: Clichy, Pigalle, the Champs Elysées, the Punch and Judy at the Luxembourg Gardens; for the last section, he went to the region around Honfleur at the mouth of the Seine. The parents' flat was a small apartment in the 18th arrondissement, and its confined space made camera manoeuvring awkward. It also impeded direct recording, as there was no room for microphone booms. But anyway, direct recording was expensive because of the multiplicity of microphones and recording equipment, and in the end Truffaut chose to post-synchronise. Some of the school scenes were shot with direct sound, and he was disappointed with the results: the background noise of Paris drowned the voices – these are the least audible parts of the film. On the other hand, the interview with the psychologist lent itself to direct recording, and came out so authentic that Truffaut regretted that cost prevented him using direct sound elsewhere. The total cost of the film was 37 million francs, precisely the same as *Le Beau Serge*, and one quarter the average at that time for a feature film.

In only one area did Truffaut relax his strict economy: he shot the film in Dyaliscope, a French equivalent of Cinemascope, requiring a special lens, the hire of which accounted for about a million francs of the final budget. He considered this a reasonable price to pay for the advantages it brought. The film was in danger of becoming ugly, even sordid: it dealt with gloomy problems in grey suburbs, with often unattractive characters. Truffaut felt that the wide-angle lens 'stylised' things and relieved some of the sense of constriction. 'With 'Scope, even emptying dustbins seems less filthy.' The cost was slightly compensated by the fact that 'Scope tends to permit, even enforce, longer and therefore fewer takes, reducing shooting time and therefore cost. The width of the image allowed the whole of the Doinels' apartment to be encompassed with the merest of pivoting movements; the action was thus broken up less, which reduced editing problems. Finally, it solved certain problems in the scenario, notably the last sequence where the image freezes on Antoine but simultaneously emphasises the immensity of the horizon behind. Truffaut felt that it was the use of 'Scope that permitted this 'visual' end, hanging delicately balanced between optimism and pessimism, either of which, stated, would have betrayed the rest of the film as well as Truffaut's reality.

If *Les Mistons* is youth remembered with a wry smile, *Les Quatre Cents Coups* is an amalgam of more sombre memories. Truffaut has said: If there is a thesis in the film, it is this: adolescence leaves a pleasant impression only in the minds of adults endowed with very bad memories.' For him, Antoine is quite specifically thirteen, the age 'of the discovery of injustice, the first unsatisfied sexual curiosities, the precocious desire for social independence, and a certain family disaffection . . . the cursed age, the age of the awakening of the conscience, and the awareness of responsibilities to be assumed . . . My film is neither optimistic nor pessimistic about this age; it is rather a personal testimony concerning a precise period of one's life.'

The long tracking shot behind the titles shows us a glum inner Paris suburb, ironically contrasted with the distant Eiffel Tower which is so insistently

Les Quatre Cent Coups: *Antoine in class, learning to be a born loser.*

present that it comes to seem almost phallic. The first scenes show Antoine's schoolroom; the oppressive life there, subtly but insistently brutalising, is reflected here in the flat greys of the film's texture. It is also mocked by the camera lingering on the school motto, *Liberté Egalité Fraternité*.

The sexual side is present in the exaggerated amount of thigh his mother seems to show when taking off her stockings, and in the consciously erotic overtones of the rubbing-down he gets after his bath, and of the privilege of getting into his parents' bed. Still too immature to cope with these awakening sensations, Antoine and his classmates seize on anything suggestive of love (in the poem, for instance) to try by their knowing reactions to suggest that they are already initiated into this foreign world.

All these embarrassing, uncomfortable aspects of life come to a head when Antoine sees his mother kissing another man. He is forced into an increased isolation and a dull acceptance of suffering. Excusing his absence from school, he lies that his mother is dead – almost a psychological truth: subjectively, the mother who has exercised such an obsessive fascination over him *has* just died, or at least he is willing her death.

One of the most impressive aspects of the portrait of Antoine is the impassive look with which he faces each new trial or accusation, and later confronts his mother's cajoling pleas. At once expressionless and expressive of a deepening distrust of the world, this impassive face renders all the more poignant the one occasion in the police van when, though Antoine's face remains fixed, we see tears trickling down his cheeks. Inured to indifference, Antoine has come to reflect it. This is also the story of an unwanted child, ignored since birth. Truffaut has referred to Emperor Frederick II's experiments in bringing up children without letting them hear a word, in order to find what language they would spontaneously speak. In fact, they all died young. For

Les Quatre Cent Coups: *Antoine's parents (Claire Maurier and Albert Rémy).*

Truffaut, Antoine is such a child who has managed to survive, deprived of all endearments, to the age of thirteen. 'He is the contrary of a maltreated child. He is not treated at all.' His mother never uses his first name, while his father talks of how to dispose of him, as if he were not present. Unwanted, he is as self-effacing as possible at home; but in compensation, away from home, he is violent and assertive.

Much of the detail in the film may not be particularly significant to the viewer, but it was highly charged for the director; a certain degree of identity between Antoine and Truffaut is immediately apparent. His friend Jacques Rivette associates at least the following aspects of the story with Truffaut himself: 'the dire consequences of a stupid lie, an abortive flight, humiliation, and the discovery of injustice'. Talking of Antoine, Truffaut suddenly breaks into the first person: 'So at thirteen I was impatient to become an adult, wanting to be able to commit all sorts of crimes without being punished for them. It seemed to me that a child's life was made up of endless infractions of some law or another, and an adult's life of simple accidents. If I broke a plate, then I hid the pieces in a rubbish-bin. Now I amuse my friends by recounting how I ran my car into a tree.'

The exact degree of autobiography of the film is uncertain, and not particularly important, since whether he is Truffaut or not, Antoine is a valid artistic creation in his own right. Truffaut has said of his more personal films that he seldom sets down exactly what he himself experienced, but works by analogy. Elsewhere though, he has said that all incidents in the film, if they didn't happen to him personally, happened to people he knew or had read about. Soon after the success of *Les Quatre Cents Coups*, he published an article entitled '*Je n'ai pas écrit ma biographie en 400 coups*', but the article itself suggests the contrary in its total effect. It seems from the line of argument he uses that it was published principally to free his parents from the serious accusations

Les Quatre Cent Coups: *Antoine, René (Patrick Auffay) and Harriet Andersson in* Summer with Monica.

Antoine's parents might well be called to answer: 'If Doinel sometimes resembles the turbulent adolescent I was, his parents resemble in no way my own, who were excellent.' While sympathising with the impulse that produced the article, one can doubt its veracity. Truffaut's family life does seem to have been grim and lonely. Certainly he did end up in the Centre de Mineurs Délinquants, at Villejuif, by the age of 16. And from this reformatory it was not his parents who rescued him, but André and Janine Bazin, just as they were to rescue him again three years later from an army prison. The film was dedicated to Bazin, who died just six months too soon to witness his protégé's success.

The spectator's sympathies are certainly with the boy, but remarkably, in a film transposing his own life, Truffaut has resisted the temptation to present a totally black and white picture, a self-justification in which all the blame is thrust on others, or on society in general. Though the parents are presented with little sympathy, there

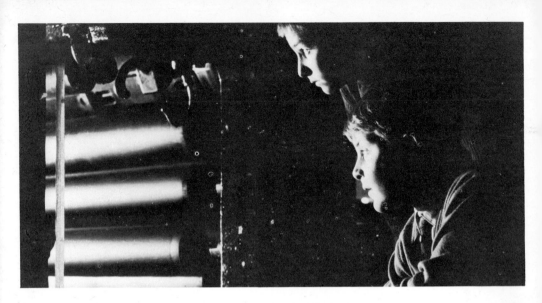

Les Quatre Cent Coups: *Antoine and René.*

are moments of genuine gaiety and communion. And it is not society in general but the too rigid application of its rules that causes Antoine to go astray. The incident of the prison van is auto-biographical; there was a law that minors should be conveyed separately and not thrust into contact with crooks and prostitutes; the law was just, but never applied, as the young Truffaut early learnt. The interview where he talks of this is worth quoting in full:

'From the moment you contest society's rights, why not go into the cinema without paying – I did that throughout my youth – by getting a pal who's paid for his seat to come and open the emergency exit for you?

That's cheating the system, which is to accept it . . .

But everyone will tell you that you must cheat in an unjust society. You can't claim the advantages of all points of view at the same time – of complicity and of contestation. To take one example: I don't believe in Justice; if then I'm insulted in a magazine, I'm not going to bring anyone up in court, since I don't believe in the courts . . .

You think, then, that society being irrevocably unjust, you must learn to live outside it?

If you like . . . you have to protect yourself. I establish barriers around me, because it's necessary if you want to survive. I don't believe that replacing some people by others will ever solve anything . . . I believe in formulae allowing a large amount of give and take, which are more or less true for people in general. But there'll always exist a disparity between a law and its application . . . For me, another society wouldn't change anything. Oppression would still be present. What you have to do, then, is survive as best you can, without letting yourself be drawn into some new group wanting self-interestedly to oppress with new ideas.'

For a man with these opinions, there must have

been a strong temptation to contrast an evil society with an innocent child whose punishments were totally unjust. Truffaut was too self-aware to fall into this trap. In preventing Léaud from smiling, he was attempting to present the facts more objectively instead of begging the question by being merely ingratiating.

Antoine is already deceitful when we first meet him, and his behaviour is a calculated blend of good and bad. Alone in the flat, he puts coal on the fire and then wipes his hands on the curtains, steals money, uses his mother's toilet things, and sets the table and then sweeps aside what he has laid to make way for his homework. If things go badly, it is at least partly his fault.

This relativity of values, the complexity of motives, shades of responsibility and incessant qualifications are an intrinsic part of the author's personality. It is a consequence of them that the film ends so equivocally in no more than a frozen moment, a moment like many others when he has opposed his impassive face – into which one can read questioning, accusation, or even bewilderment – to the fortuitous developments of his life. Yet it is also consistent with previous occasions when the sea has been presented as a symbol of escape and freedom. Now, fleeing from the reformatory, Antoine has finally breasted the last sand-dunes and arrived at the wide horizon of the ocean. Yet once at the water, he is uncertain as to what to do next. The absolutes, the ideals, which reaching the sea has symbolised for him, disintegrate once the gesture is achieved – a further element in the growing-up process underlying the film: Antoine is learning to accept the lack of any real certainties in life, the absence of any definitive and permanent achievements. One might read into that expression-less face a degree of disillusionment and a struggle to adjust to a developing comprehension of life. Yet, as Jacques Doniol-Valcroze has said, it is doubtful if the future will be as bad as the past: there is a feeling of having 'come through', of having survived a *'voyage au bout de la nuit'*. Whatever happens, 'a great discovery has been made containing the germs of moral beauty and generosity.'

If the sea has represented an absolute ideal, a

distant goal, there is a more immediate means of escape from Antoine's sordid surroundings: the cinema. Acting out Truffaut's own youth, Antoine seizes every opportunity to plunge into the cinema, to immerse himself in another, more exciting world. As for the young Truffaut, the exact nature of the film is irrelevant. Those Antoine attends are pretty sensational stuff: white-slaving on the first occasion, with an affectionate pan upwards to frame the sign CINE; a monster film on the second, when they steal a poster. And as if by accident, they are always posing in front of, or just passing, walls covered with movie posters. Even Antoine's outing with his parents, their one moment of human contact, is a visit to the cinema.

The obsession is present in less obvious ways. When Antoine enters the rotor in the fairground – a scene Truffaut qualifies in the scenario with the word *'Extase'* – the flickering of the faces round the rim of the revolving drum recreates the system on which many early experiments in animation were based. He also included references to some favourite directors, particularly to Rossellini and Vigo, in his opinion the only ones who had managed to recreate the world of childhood as he was hoping to. This helps explain many scenes that may seem, and often are, irrelevant to the main line of the plot. What he mainly admired in Rossellini's *Germania, anno zero* was the gravity of the children's world. The Vigo references are more specific. The school and prison scenes where children are marched about to repeated whistle blasts deliberately echo *Zéro de conduite*. So do some of the incidents in the classroom, like the master's gesture in removing his spectacles. Another reference is the children's crack about the passing priest, *'Bonjour Madame'*; in Vigo, the teacher, following an attractive woman, gets side-tracked by the skirts of the priest, who is similarly disconcerted. Equally, the class that leaves the school door as a group of thirty and slowly diminishes to three is reminiscent of the crocodile that disintegrates in Vigo, only to reconstitute itself on arrival back at school. However, it is also a personal memory: 'We used to leave school (near the rue des Martyrs) to go to the stadium, but at the stadium there were never more than 10 or 12 of the 30 pupils that started out . . . I wanted to include this episode because it was silent, visual, and readily appreciable.' There is also a basic difference from Vigo which stems from Truffaut's preference for experienced reality rather than fantasy or idealism: Vigo had his characters clearly divided into the pure and the evil. He even rejected at the last minute an 'evil' character in the schoolboy's camp on the grounds that he tended to confuse the battle-lines. In *Les Quatre Cent Coups*, Truffaut has just such a character in Moricet.

The 'personal notations' do more than just give the film consistency. They also give it a certain unpredictability, as so many of the scenes are unexplained and seem unjustified. The carefully sliced-up banana skin, the surrealistic decorations of Renés family home, the medical discussion between the old women, the pinball machine, the sudden appearance of the two boys on either side of a young girl whom we don't know and never meet again – all these, though they can sometimes be related to the themes and were often more fully explained in the original scenario, have in the film the totally fortuitous feel, the arbitrariness of living.

This contrasts strongly with the intricately plotted scenarios of the 'quality tradition', where painstakingly counter-pointed plotlines converge to a climax and where every shot is aimed to be directly relevant. Here many scenes could be left out; others could be included (and indeed were intended to be). The total impact of the film would not be greatly different for these changes, since the atmosphere and the personality that they contributed to build up would still be the same.

As well as liking the cinema, Truffaut also admired certain authors, and they are quoted as readily as the directors he admired. When the children pass a wall with GIRAUDOUX scrawled on it, we can be sure it is not by accident. Similarly, Balzac is quoted, not only here by Truffaut but also by Chabrol and Godard. It is appropriate that 'La Recherche de l'absolu' arouses Antoine's admiration, further evidence of the same craving which drives him towards the sea at the end.

Shooting began on 10 November 1958 and was finished by 5 January 1959, less than fifty days later. It was selected as part of the French contingent for Cannes Film Festival; presented there on 18 May, it won first prize for direction. The *President d'honneur* of the jury was Jean Cocteau, whom Cahiers had always regarded with admiration as a true *auteur de cinema*. He also had dealt with *enfants terribles,* and Truffaut quotes him respectfully when talking about Antoine: 'As the death penalty did not exist in schools, Dargelos was sent down.' With his well-known penchant for encouraging young talent, it was natural that Cocteau should be enthusiastic about *Les Quatre Cents Coups*. In photographs from the festival he can be seen beaming benevolently at Truffaut, or with his arm around Léaud's shoulders. He gave

Cannes Film Festival, 1959: Léaud and Truffaut lionized by Jean Cocteau and French society.

Léaud a small part in *Le Testament d'Orphée* the following year. Truffaut says that when making *Les Quatre Cents Coups* he was aware the Bigey's apartment was *à la Cocteau*, especially the stuffed horse and the grotesque decorations. The scene where the children flap the covers to clear away the smoke also recalls *Les Enfants Terribles,* and 'I think this is the point where Cocteau really began to appreciate the film'.

The film was an immediate success. Normally restrained magazines and literary supplements devoted most of their front pages to it, and when it opened in Paris on 3 June, its popularity was assured. It collected at least fifteen prizes in the following year, including, surprisingly enough, the Catholic O.C.I.C. prize. With the insulted curé censored out by the distributors, it could indeed be said to show 'the suffering endured in an irreligious environment, where the family ties were consequently weakened'.

Cannes, 1959: Truffaut and his young star dine with the Président d'Honneur.

Some valid criticisms were nevertheless made, notably about the acting and about inconsistencies in tone. Albert Rémy who plays Antoine's father is excellent, but René is merely adequate in a colourless role while Antoine's mother and René's father are unacceptable. In a film in which such efforts are made to achieve a feeling of realism, the schoolchildren's group scenes look very rehearsed. The breaking of Moricet's glasses, for instance, has as little spontaneity as a religious rite, though of course Vigo intentionally played up the ritual element in the schoolroom scenes even more.

The only aspect of the film consistently criticised in reviews was the music: it was too 'jaunty' for the context. This saddened Truffaut, for as an assiduous attender of music-hall and cabaret, he had long admired Jean Constantin. He had even intended to create a role for him in the film, but as it was already too long, he never shot Constantin's scenes. He explains the clash of styles by saying that when he asked Constantin to do the music, he still thought the film would be quite gay. It became progressively sadder in the course of shooting because the child's problems assumed a greater significance. So although he is still satisfied with the result, he admits that perhaps Constantin wasn't the right man for the film as it ended up.

On the other hand, the achievements are immense. He had avoided all the intellectual games, the emotional cheating he had attacked so strongly in others, and put into practice the principles he propounded over the preceding years: independence through cheapness, and a use of the ensuing liberty to expose genuine problems, to recreate believable characters in real situations. His film was one of the signs of a renewal in the French cinema; it came directly after Chabrol's *Le Beau Serge* and *Les Cousins,* three months before Godard's *A bout de souffle*, and appeared at Cannes in the same festival as Alain Resnais's *Hiroshima mon amour*. Unlike the films of Chabrol and Godard, Truffaut's films were to become progressively cooler – as *L'Enfant Sauvage* reveals – perhaps because, for him, injustice was a simple fact of life and as such could be stated simply. Talking of other directors whose style involves this same *'douceur terrible'*, this restrained presentation of the unacceptable, Truffaut expresses admiration of Resnais's *Nuit et brouillard* and Franju's *La Tête contre les murs*, but emphasises that Franju is fascinated by abnormal situations, by the *insolite,* whereas he prefers the factual, the product of his own experience. As in the work of both directors and of Renoir, whom he admires so much, the more emotional impact is inherent in a situation, the more discretion he shows in filming it: *'plus la matière est émouvante, moins il faut chercher à émouvoir.'*

On viewing a finished film, one tends to see it as the inevitable outcome of the author's intentions. In fact, of course, changes are made continually right up to the moment of shooting and then continue under a different name – improvisation. As the final version of the scenario happens to be extant, we can see how far Truffaut was willing to adapt his ideas.

The scenario calls for the credits to unfold against a closed desk-top, which is to open for the pin-up incident, thus opening the film. Accompanying the subsequent classroom scenes, and many later ones, is a commentary spoken by an older René, recalling his schooldays and his companion Antoine. It starts: 'The paradise lost of childhood is an invention of old men. How can one still believe in it at eighteen? . . . Our thirteenth year dragged on and on . . . Antoine Loinod remembers it all too well: for him it was the time of injustice.' In feeling, this recalls *Les Mistons*, and is evidently a relic of the film's origin as a companion piece. The commentary was progressively eliminated, with the beneficial result (and probably the intention) of making the themes less overt. Instead of being spelled out in the commentary, themes, opinions and character traits are presented visually to the spectator in the action but not forced on him. The quote is also a reminder that Antoine's name throughout the scenario was Loinod not Doinel as it became in the film. (Doniol in reverse; Doniol-Valcroze acted under the name Etienne Loinod in Rivette's *Le Coup du berger*.)

Next come several playground scenes, with talk between masters of a possible strike, all mention of which was omitted from the final version. Then René comes home with Antoine to help with his homework; they go shopping, lose the list and buy the wrong food. Instead, the film concentrates here on Antoine alone in the house, establishing his character by the 'carefully judged mixture of good and bad'. In the scenario, many place-names are mentioned, suburb and street names being specified, even precise buildings and doorways designated – an added suggestion of the film's relevance to Truffaut's own life, as is the affectionate mention of two boulevard cinemas: 'It was there, in that atmosphere purified by night and by DDT, that the adventure began.' The film to be seen by the children is not specified; we are simply told they are to indulge in 'dialogue appropriate to the film projected (heroism and sudden justice)'. There was also to have been an amusing incident with a passing provincial, played by Raymond Devos (who later appeared as the man on the landing-stage in *Pierrot le fou*). In the fairground episode, 'the camera will emphasise the monstrous and disproportionate aspect of modern gaiety, interplay of metallic elements, whirling round abouts, rockets of steel, etc.' – a satirical element that has also

disappeared.

Later, when Antoine's father tells him he should show more initiative, the directions indicate flash shots of Antoine's memories of the rotor. Similar flash shots were to accompany the reading of Balzac, but are replaced in the final version by a close-up of the page. Wandering around Paris, Antoine was to witness several odd tableaux including a man stooping to peer through a church door 'as if to watch the mass through a key-hole'. These obsessive personal memories or references may have been filmed but were not included in the final version. Most remarkable, the time Antoine

Les Quatre Cent Coups: *Antoine as the hooligan element in the police station.*

Les Quatre Cent Coups: *top left: Truffaut recalls Zéro de conduite; top right: the indignities of finger-printing; bottom: emotion gets the better of Antoine.*

spends in René's house was fully treated in some fourteen pages (about a seventh of the scenario). There is a little girl who makes a fuss and is left at home by her parents. She creates an uproar, which disturbs all the neighbours. Antoine and René feed her and a boy who lives opposite performs a play for her. As our heroes have given her their own meal, they fabricate a new one of 'caramel' in a saucepan. Then they go on to get the cats drunk. René's mother hides Antoine whose father has come to look for him but René's father, who is more fully delineated than in the film, tells Antoine he must leave.

All that remains of this is a fragment of the caramel-making, and the blanket-flapping scene. The rest, lovingly detailed in the scenario, has all been cut, perhaps because the girl or René's father proved inadequate as actors, but perhaps also because the film, already over-long, needed to be trimmed of personal references at this point. In contrast, the detention scenes have all been greatly expanded to give them more weight as they contribute directly to building up the climax. The material omitted would have explained the behaviour of René's family and the abrupt appearance of the little girl; the film would have lost some elements of its arbitrariness at the expense of gaining others. Truffaut has had to try achieving the same effect more rapidly and with less material.

The typewriter scene is detailed minutely in the scenario, and sounds authentic. The building and firm are specified. The hat incident, however, is absent. The prosecution scenes have not merely been expanded but considerably modified: Antoine originally remained in the cell with a group of crooks and prostitutes, who treated him with a certain camaraderie. The trip to the reformatory is referred to as simply three scenes of a police van in the streets at night. No indication is given of Antoine's tears, there is no mention elsewhere of the expressionlessness of his face. Léaud's acting ability seems to have suggested wider possibilities as shooting progressed.

This hypothesis is reinforced by the scenes with the psychologist who, we are told, was to have been a young woman, quite pretty and wearing glasses. The camera was to have stayed on her, as we heard Antoine's answers 'off'. In the film, though, we never see her; instead there are the magnificent shots of Antoine's 'explanations'. Truffaut explains how this happened: he was worried that the psychologist's questions too closely resembled those in *Chiens Perdus sans collier,* but didn't know what to do about it. Then he had difficulty finding an actress for the part, and realised that the characteristics he had in mind exactly fitted the script-writer Annette Wademant, who was not in Paris at the time – hence the decision to shoot just Léaud's side of the interview, and add her side when she became available. Truffaut discussed the interview with the boy, explaining in general what sort of questions he

would ask, but left him free to answer in his own words, hoping to achieve a certain spontaneity. To make it easier for Léaud, he formulated questions which applied both to Antoine and to Léaud himself, merely asking him not to contradict the rest of the scenario. He shot the scene with no one in the room except Léaud himself and the cameraman Decaë. When they saw the rushes, Decaë suggested that they should leave it as it was, adding only the voice of the psychologist. This they did, though they retained only three of the twenty minutes shot.

There follow scenes in which Antoine's mother visits a fortune-teller. These were omitted as a possible distraction from Antoine at the climactic moment. When René tries to contact Antoine at the reformatory, Truffaut specifies that the books he brings are copies of Cinémonde, and that the guard tosses them away because they're not food. It is totally irrelevant, since we're never near enough to see them, yet curiously endearing, for this is precisely what Truffaut's friend Robert Lachenay would have tried to bring him.

The final escape was to involve a flight through changing countryside and a ride in the back of a truck. The film version is once again more coherent and dramatic, since it complies with the unities of time and space. The final lines of the projected scenario indicate:

'107. He will stop only when the foam comes and soaks the soles of his shoes.
108. The last image of that scene, Antoine at the seaside, becomes fixed and fades into another moving image: Antoine and René walking through the streets of Paris and this image in turn becomes fixed, reminding us that it is taken by a street photographer, whilst we hear the last words of René's commentary: "Thus it was that I received a postcard from Fontenoy-sur-Mer, where I managed to contact Antoine. How are we doing now? Fine, thank you . . . and yourself? We are free, and far from the torments of adolescence, but as we wander through the streets we can't help feeling a certain complicity with our successors, too, as we watch them *recommencer Les Quatre Cents Coups*".'

In the film, however, this final image and

commentary have been cut, and the whole last sequence is transformed. We are no longer looking back from a safe distance, with an older René, at something that turned out satisfactorily, a cycle that will repeat with each generation. On the contrary, we see it from Antoine's viewpoint – disconcerted, unaware of what the future will bring, conditioned to expect the worst. Truffaut's later description of the final shots significantly ends on a question: 'Running through the fields, he arrives at last face to face with the sea which he has never seen before. Reconciled with nature, will he soon also be reconciled with life?'

It seems safe to say that the scenario was used only for reference. Less than half of it remains in the film. Since he had never before undertaken the transformation from scenario into film on such a scale, Truffaut was willing to reject anything which, on realisation turned out to be inappropriate to the actors' personalities or the precise location. Much of the scenario was certainly shot but rejected later on for various reasons. In this sense, Truffaut relied heavily on improvisation. The scenario gives no stage directions, camera movements, or décors. These would depend solely on cost and availability. Very sensibly, Truffaut approached his first film tentatively, as an experiment.

When the film was reissued in 1967 Truffaut made some changes, adding eight minutes. He says that when he made it he was afraid to exceed the magic one-and-a-half-hour limit. He managed to keep within five minutes of it only by the strictest editing. The restored material removed some ambiguities: in the 1959 version we never found out what happened to M. Loinod's Guide Michelin; we might reasonably have surmised that Mme Loinod had taken it. The scenes where Antoine is seen tearing it up to make pellets remove this doubt. He also extended the early scenes establishing the boys' personalities and restored certain sections which had been unofficially censored. The boys' calling the curé 'Madame' had shocked some Catholics, and had been cut out by the distributors. In some foreign versions the end

had been made less pessimistic with a spoken commentary, perhaps like the one Truffaut himself had removed.

The film must have had an effect on Truffaut himself, in representing some kind of exorcism of much of his past life. Doniol-Valcroze says that 'making the film reconciled Truffaut to life in somewhat the same way as reaching the sea reconciles Antoine to life' – without signifying any final resolution. A long-imagined dream had been realised, and now it was necessary to adjust to the idea of it as merely a stepping-stone.

THE SESSION WITH THE PSYCHOLOGIST IN THE SCENARIO:

She is young and quite pretty, and wears glasses. Nervously, she lights each cigarette from the butt of the last.

PSYCHOLOGIST: Come in. Don't be afraid. And above all don't think of this as a test. Not at all. I simply want us to get to know one another. Your name is Antoine Loinod, and you're 13½, right? (*No reply.*) Answer at least yes or no.

ANTOINE: (Inaudibly) Yes.

P: To begin with you can tell me what this picture means to you. Look closely. Don't worry. (*Picture of an old man dragging a cart, circa 1900.*)

A: (*Off*) Don't know.

P: Your eyes all right?

A: Yes.

P: Good, now this one. (*Picture of a dignified old man with a young girl, on a seat.*)

A: (*Off*) Don't know.

P: Of course you know. You'll be here for ever if you keep this up.

A: Like the rest, it's just a mess.

P: That's all?

A: Yes.

P: And what about this third picture? (*Picture of a prisoner.*)

A: (*After a long time*) A delinquent, same place, a little later.

[*Non sequitur. Presumably a line missing:* Repeat after me 1/5/3/0/9/4.]

A: (*Very quickly*) 1/5/3/0/9/4.

P: 8/7/3/5/0/6.

A: 8/7/3/5/0/6.

P: 7/3/0/6/2/9/8.

A: 7/3/0/6/2/9/8.

P: Good. Now it's a sentence I want you to repeat. Listen closely. (*She reads.*) The underground is cheaper than the bus . . . Sorry, I mean the omnibus. I'll say that again. The underground is cheaper than the omnibus. It only costs . . . (*10fr is written; she mentally corrects*) twenty francs. It's strange in Paris to see women there driving taxis. (*Antoine tries a cheeky smile.*)

P: (*Seeing his smile*) Repeat.

A: The underground is cheaper than the omnibus. (*Antoine is drawing; the psychologist watches him closely; he holds out his drawing to her, it shows his father, his mother, and himself – at least we can suppose it is of them.*)

P: Thank you. Now I'm going to read you some stories. At the end of each story I'll ask you a question. Are you ready?

A: (*Absently*) Yes.

P: A father and a mother bird and their little baby bird are asleep in a nest on a branch. (*Antoine sees this as an animated cartoon; her voice continues off.*) But suddenly a wind gets up, it shakes the trees, and the nest falls to the ground. The three birds are woken up sharply. The father flies quickly to a fir tree, the mother to another. What does the little bird do? It can already fly a little. (*As soon as she asks the question, the camera frames the psychologist.*)

A: (*Eyes glazed*) It makes the most of it and goes off with a pal.

P: Right. Now another . . . (*She ferrets about amongst her papers.*) A boy comes home from school (or a walk) and his mother says to him: don't do your homework right away. I've got something to tell you. What is she going to say?

A: Go and do the shopping.

Cut to Scene 98 (Antoine's mother at the fortune-teller). Then . . .

P: But how did you find out?

A: I talked to René about it. He's my pal and he told me to check the Family Allowance book. So one evening, when no one was home, I looked.

P: And that gave you a bit of a shock.

A: No.

P: What . . . you found out your dad wasn't your real father, and it doesn't mean anything to you?

A: Oh me, I thought it was more likely my mother wasn't my real mother.

P: Why . . .? (*A pause*) Tell me why. (*He bursts into tears.*)

IN THE FILM:

P: . (*Off*) Why did you bring back the typewriter?

A: Well . . . because . . . well I couldn't sell it, you see . . . couldn't do anything with it . . . I got scared . . . I don't know, I brought it back . . . don't know why . . . just did.

P: (*Off*) Tell me, is it true you stole ten thousand francs from your grandmother?

A: She asked me in, it was her birthday . . . and anyway, you see, she's old, she doesn't eat much . . . and she hoards up all her money . . . she'd never have needed it; she was going to die soon . . . Well, I knew where she stashed it, so I went and swiped it . . . just coins, you know. I knew she'd never notice it. Proof is, she didn't; she gave me a smashing book that day. Well then, my mother used to go through my pockets, and that evening I left my pants on the bed. I suppose she came and took the money, because next day it wasn't there. Then she asked me about it and I had to admit I'd taken it from my grandmother. Well then she confiscated this book my grandmother had given me. One day I asked for it back, because I wanted to read it, and I found she'd sold it.

P: (*Off*) Your parents say you tell lies all the time.

A: Well I tell lies, I suppose. I tell lies from time to time, you know . . . sometimes even if I told the truth they wouldn't believe it, so it's easier to tell lies.

P: Why don't you love your mother?

A: Because first I was looked after by a nurse . . . and when they had a bit of money, they sent me to my grandmother . . . my grandmother, she got old and that . . . she couldn't keep me . . . so I went back to my parents, I was eight then . . . you know . . . I noticed my mother, she didn't like me much . . . she was always on at me, and for no reason . . . for nothing at all . . . well then I . . . when . . . when there was a row in the house one day I . . . I heard that . . . that my mother had had me when she was . . . when she . . . before she was married, you know . . . and then she had a row with my grandmother once . . . and that's when I found out . . . she'd wanted to have me aborted, and if I was born it's only because of my grandmother . . .

P: What do you think of your father?

A: Oh, my father, he's OK you know . . . but he's a bit of a coward, because . . . oh, he knows my mother's running round with other men, only, not to have a row . . . he just . . . just rather not say anything . . . let things go . . .

P: Have you ever slept with a girl?

A: (*Tentative, knowing smile*) No, never, but . . . well I know some kids who've . . . who've done it . . . they told me if you really want to, you've just got to go to the rue St. Denis. So I went . . . so I asked some of the women there, got myself really told off . . . so I got the shits. Then I went back a couple of times, though. Then once I was standing there and a bloke saw me and said . . . he knew the women pretty well I think, 'cos he said 'I know this girl . . . you know, who takes . . . this girl . . . takes on kids, and that . . .' well he took me to this hotel where she was . . . but that day she just wasn't there, so we waited . . . an hour . . . two, maybe . . . she didn't come . . . I upped and left . . .

Tirez sur le pianiste

The Cannes festival of 1959 had been a triumph for young directors and established the New Wave both in France and internationally. But this very popularity was disconcerting for Truffaut, who had believed that he was making a film for a small group of enthusiasts. Instead he found that his film had been taken up by the mass public 'who only go to the cinema twice a year to see fashionable films'. Interpretations were distorting it, and it began to seem very remote to him. Success had other effects, too: 'What is important, now I come to think of it, is that after Cannes I bought a car. One day I said to myself "Well, well, it's six months since I took the Metro." And that's serious. But if I took the Metro "just to see", that would be even more ridiculous . . . In four years I will be incapable of making another film like it because I'll have forgotten that sort of flat, and how it feels to put out rubbish bins, and so on.'

Even his intolerance of films which didn't meet his high standards was becoming modified, as he admits with disarming frankness: 'After a few years of criticism, I felt I had the cinema at my fingertips. I could distinguish the good from the bad and understood it all. Now I'm making films myself, I no longer know anything about it: I haven't any criteria or any principles left, I haven't the slightest idea what I'm talking about.' And elsewhere: 'I've become more indulgent, lost all intention to reform the cinema. Bad films don't arouse my indignation as they once did. I'm simply left with the determination to make good ones. I've lost the purism of the true cinemaniac; I've become an egotist, like all directors.'

Truffaut was well aware that his second film was a perilous undertaking. For all the group,

Tirez sur le pianiste: *Charlie (Charles Aznavour) at the grand piano in concert.*

their first films had been a natural choice, for economic or personal reasons, but, with producers now ready to back any film they might choose to make, the question was what direction their development should take. 'Everything is said in the first film; after that, all you do is embroider it.' Truffaut had, in rough form, several other scenarios

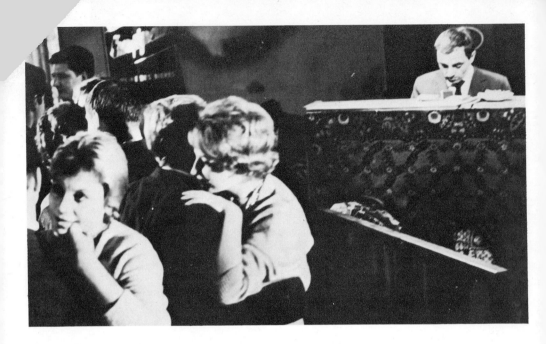

Tirez sur le pianiste: *Charlie at the honky-tonk in concert.*

about childhood and his own experiences, but decided not to persevere with them in case he seemed to be exploiting a success. Besides, he was by nature reluctant to let himself be categorised, and wanted his next film to be as different from the first as possible. He also began to feel that it was bad to be too sure of what one was going to do next: better leave it to chance and the inspiration of the moment.

In this case, the inspiration was provided by one of Marcel Camus's statements after the success of *Orfeu Negro,* also at the Cannes festival. Camus claimed that, in order to make the film he wanted, he'd had to hold out against fifteen offers of gangster films. The implied slight on gangster films infuriated Truffaut, who once estimated he had seen about 1500 of them. He had also been disconcerted to see how thoroughly French his first film had turned out to be, when his film background was mainly American. Now he acknowledged this debt by adapting a gangster story to a French setting. There was a precedent in the pre-war gangster films of Marcel Carné and Jacques Prévert, which he had admired precisely because they used the genre as a medium for a new type of realism and to express Prévert's personal preoccupations. More recently he had praised *Touchez pas au grisbi* for similar reasons. Noting that Jacques Becker was forty-eight when he made it, and Simenon forty-nine when he wrote it, he suggested that the true subject of this apparently straight-forward gangster film was 'the feeling of approaching the age of fifty'. Becker had played down the violence and the more sensational aspects

Tirez sur le pianiste: *Charlie's confidence is low.*

of the underworld, stressing instead the themes of friendship and ageing. Truffaut proposed to do something similar, and offered Pierre Braunberger a film based on David Goodis's *'Down There'*.

Truffaut felt this was a natural reaction after making an intensely personal film. His impulse to retreat into anonymity was heightened by the flood of 'personal' films in 1959, sparked off by *A bout de souffle* and *Hiroshima*. This alternation of autobiographical scenarios with adaptations was later to

Tirez sur le pianiste: *Charlie.*

become almost a matter of principle. Besides, he said, 'if I made a film each year from an original scenario, my films would all be too French, too full of nuances, too much a collection of little things, with not enough action; so with my taste for filming events which, important or not, are dramatic, I turn to books. I feel like filming their dramatic events, but would never have the courage to invent them.'

Goodis had long been one of his favourite *Série Noire* authors, and Truffaut had already been struck by the cinematic possibilities of the overnight car journey into the snow-clad mountains, which was to remain the central image. The hero is a musician of Armenian extraction which immediately suggested Charles Aznavour. Truffaut had wanted to use him since seeing him in Franju's *La Tête contre les murs,* which he named the best film of the previous year. He was later attacked for building a film around such a well-known personality, going back, it seemed, on principles which had led him to deride the 'star system'. For him, however, stars (like big budgets) had never been bad in themselves, but only insofar as they tended to undermine the director's control. He would never make a film with Michèle Morgan, Fernandel, Gérard Philipe, Jean Gabin or Pierre Fresnay because they saw films as vehicles for projecting their own image, and would 'correct' anything in the film that didn't correspond to their inclinations. Aznavour's attitude was entirely different; he was willing to abide by a director's decisions. Because her attitude was similar, Truffaut chose to work with Jeanne Moreau in his next film. Besides, Renoir – his guide in so many things – had often built films around stars, though usually the more attractive female ones. Perhaps not the least important reason for wanting Aznavour was the curious physical resemblance between him and Truffaut. Just as Léaud was to grow to resemble Truffaut to a disturbing extent, Aznavour already looked like a slightly more care-worn version of him.

The preparation and shooting of the scenario did not proceed entirely smoothly. Truffaut could not take seriously, or commit himself to, the fundamental situations of the genre. It began to seem to him that underworld conventions and attitudes were simply those of any bourgeois society, very slightly modified – 'gangsters who are fathers, and who gasp "look after my kids", or "see my wife gets the money", etc. I quite like people in society, provided they are alone; not if they organise themselves into a gang . . .' In fact he was becoming aware of an attitude that was to unite all his films: the protagonists are brought into conflict with the existing order of things and were to be outsiders who champion a society in which the individual is more free to express himself. He said, possibly exaggerating a little: 'I'm interested mainly in thieves, beggars – and prostitutes, the asocial people of whom I should least like to see society cleansed.. Anyway, would it want to be . . . ?' As a result, during shooting he emphasised more and more Aznavour's solitude. Lena remarks, 'Even when he's with other people, he's alone'. Conversely, he treated those gangster scenes that remained in a slightly jocular fashion: 'I got out of the problem not by parody but by a sort of drollery. Really I was very ill at ease making it.'

His gangsters are highly original creations, slightly grotesque yet also disarmingly human and down-to-earth: whoever saw gangsters dancing around flapping their arms to keep warm, whoever heard of a gangster's car breaking down, or saw them struggling to push it to a garage while the kidnap victim steers, bouncing up and down with excitement? Ernest can scarcely drive, and Chico knocks himself out running into a lamp-post. And surely the slang is a bit too colourful, as if the script-writer had been more intent on amusing himself than on creating characters? It all reveals a desire to break out of the genre, too constricting for Truffaut; it was neither as amusing nor as appropriate to his personality as he had thought. Even the gun battle at the end, the inevitable show-down, is distinctly grotesque, distorted, so that the gangsters appear fallible and slightly ludicrous human beings trying desperately to act out traditional gangster situations in a convincing manner.

And yet, these purely burlesque scenes are juxtaposed with moments of pure pathos. Immediately after the comic gun battle Charlie and his young brother bend over the heroine, poignantly closing her eyes. Intercut with the comic kidnapping trip is Charlie and Lena's overnight journey to the snow-clad mountains. Burlesque alternates with solemn moments of tranquillity and beauty. It is presumably the element of beauty that tempted Truffaut to say that his treatment of the story was like a *Conte de Perrault*, that is, a sort of fairy-tale, raising Charlie's vain search for love to the level of a fable.

But the result is a 'shocking' and quite deliberate confusion of genres: 'I know there seem to be four or five films crammed into this one, but it's deliberate, as I strove above all to shatter the idea of genre. I know there is nothing the public detests so much as changes of tone, but I've always had a passion for them.' Elsewhere he adds 'the tone of the film resembles a hot-and-cold shower. This is its experimental aspect. I've tried a few risky juxtapositions, alternating passages of riotous fun with others that are disgustingly melancholy. I don't think I could ever make a film all on the same level.' It is probable, too, that Truffaut got a certain malicious pleasure out of confusing the spectators, by changing the rules in mid-game, for one of his principal complaints about the previous generation had been that they made the same film over and over again, with the result that the audience could read script-writers' minds and foresee the next scenes. Here was his chance to catch them out with the unpredictable, to lead them up the garden path.

Revolting against the finished perfection of the 'quality' French tradition, Truffaut asks for the same grainy, grey, deliberately ugly image that Godard was to give to *Les Carabiniers* and *Bande à part*. On the other hand, the photography in the mountains is suitably poetic, with clear images and splendid black patterns on the snowy land-scape. This recalls the contrast between the seedy, grey, slum-like appearance of the city on the plains, symbolising hopelessness, and the purity of the mountains, symbolising fulfilment, that Rohmer later used in *Ma Nuit chez Maud*. It also recalls

Tirez sur le pianiste: *Theresa (Nicole Berger) and Charlie: flashbacks to former marital bliss and anxiety.*

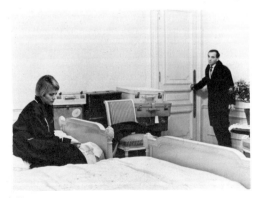

the end of *Les Quatre Cents Coups*, except that here the snow has replaced the sea as a symbol of liberation. We find that Antoine was justified in feeling ill at ease and uncertain on reaching the sea, for in the present film Charlie's similar hopes of reconciliation with life – through the 'love of a good woman' – are totally shattered; he is doomed to return from the heights to his seedy bistro and, by implication, to re-live with the new waitress the same hopeless dream he has lived out with the first, and with his wife, who was also a waitress. The message is even clearer than in the previous film: ideals are illusory, and entertaining them can only be harmful. But whereas *Les Quatre Cents Coups* embodied this message in a basically optimistic form, the overall tone of *Tirez sur le pianiste* is pessimistic.

The black and white of the photography is used to reinforce the latent meaning. In *Les Quatre Cents Coups*, Antoine had 'happened' to drink his stolen milk in front of a winter sports poster and another one advertising Chaplin's *Goldrush*, a combination suggesting his youth, innocence, and idealism. In *Tirez sur le pianiste* it is a milk-bomb, not a water-bomb, that Fido drops on the gangsters' car; and the forces of evil, normally associated with black, are hampered by this whiteness which prefigures the snow at the end.

A discussion of love and friendship is also central to the film; it forms in fact, a 'third film' imposed on the two already described. The pre-occupation with individuals and their relationships is as typical of Truffaut's private life as of his films. Antoine and René portrayed an existing friendship, as had *Les mistons*; and, in *Tirez sur le pianiste*, we again find the protagonist involved in a series of close personal relationships – three are with women, and one with his younger brother. They don't constitute any deep analysis of affection: Charlie's marriage to Teresa and the collapse of their relationship contain nothing original, and the ideal she represented in his intensely romantic imagination can be defined in simple terms. He sees in Lena the hope of realising the same ideal. Based on abstract concepts, these relationships don't lend themselves to psychological complexity. Truffaut is less interested in psychology than in noting external behaviour and his attempted psychological explanation at the close of the flash-back is no more convincing than the flashback itself, which is too long, and unrelieved by the burlesque treatment we find elsewhere in the film. It is as if Truffaut were trapped by some private significance into taking seriously material that doesn't merit it. The third variation on this theme is Charlie's relationship with Clarisse, the prostitute with a heart of gold, a stock situation.

But the subject's importance for Truffaut is shown by the introduction of Fido, who didn't appear in the book. Played by the boy in *Les Quatre Cents Coups* who kept having to tear smudged pages out of his notebook, he becomes the pivot of the action: affection for him has kept Charlie going after his wife's death, and through him the gangsters trace Charlie's mountain hide-out. It may reflect the relationship between Bazin and Truffaut which was originally to have played

a much larger part in the film.

Even more remarkable than these instances are the occasions when one of the characters pauses almost in mid-action to deliver an impromptu and apparently gratuitous aside on the subject. The casual meeting at the beginning between Chico and the stranger is used to introduce a charmingly irrelevant discussion of married love, the proportion of virgins in Paris, and the possible effects of a first child on a marriage. Truffaut and his wife had

Tirez sur le pianiste: *Charlie's kid brother Fido (Richard Kanayan) in the snow.*

had their first child earlier that year. Similarly, Plyne, while trying to strangle Charlie, delivers himself of thoughts on ideal love and the Purity of Womanhood – ludicrous in context, but not fundamentally different from ideals that Charlie seeks in his women. The mysterious stranger makes the same kind of declaration at the end of *Baisers Volés*. A final variation on the theme is provided by Ernest's lecherous soliloquy during the drive, beginning with his father who had been run over through watching women instead of cars (and had died through trying to grab a passing nurse), and passing on to several dubious puns and cynical epigrams. Truffaut pointed out that love was the one unifying element of the film – 'the men in it speak of nothing but women, and the women of nothing but men. At the height of the pay-off or the kidnapping the only thing they speak of is Love – sexual, romantic, physical, moral, social, conjugal . . .'.

Reluctantly the focus of all these relationships, Charlie is a typical Goodis hero and has particular relevance to Truffaut. Goodis's novels reveal an obsession with moral culpability, a certain masochism, an awareness of original sin and a puritanical distrust of physical love; his ill-fated heroes aim at escaping the world of action and achieve a state of passivity, or solitary indifference. The pianist is no exception, but the interest lies in Truffaut's modifications. Although he jokingly admits to being puritanical, he makes love to no less than three women in the course of the film, and with enthusiasm. None of these scenes is taken from the book, and they are regrettably trite, especially that in which Charlie goes to bed with Lena.

Truffaut also used the analogy of Charlie's musical talent to speak of his own artistic hopes and fears. He mentions his new-found wealth and success, and continues: 'Probably I'm not a great artist, but I need someone to believe I am.' His wife replies: 'I'd prefer you to be pretentious, and certain of your genius. The least criticism makes you ill, but after all why should you worry, and anyway you weren't any too gentle with others, not so long ago . . .' This obviously refers to Truffaut's career as a critic, and it's amusing to hear Charlie reply 'Exactly: I rather regret all that!' 'Ah, ah', she says, 'regrets; too late, my man!' This all corresponds to Truffaut's own admissions of critical humility at this period.

Charlie's lack of self-confidence is another theme contributed solely by Truffaut. The original Eddie was a tough character with strong masochistic impulses. Charlie is quite the reverse. Plyne recognises his timidity, Clarisse thinks him timid (at least until the episode under the sheet), and it is the timidity of his joke rather than the joke itself that makes gangsters laugh. His hesitation in taking Lena's hand confirms all this, and our later discovery that Lena was equally anguished at the time does suggest a world peopled with tentative, uncertain individuals wanting simply to make contact but seldom daring to try. The feeling is reinforced by Charlie's nervous hesitation at the impresario's door. The camera suddenly retreats to the other end of the corridor, from which point Charlie looks small, trapped, and very much alone.

He overcomes his timidity twice. In a scene improvised during shooting the impresario advises him that shyness is an illness and should be treated as such: Charlie buys books on the subject and we see him facing journalists with new-found confidence. The second occasion is the psychological climax of the plot: he has walked to the piano to avoid getting involved in a confrontation with Plyne. It looks as if his defeatist impulses will win out: 'You can't do anything for Plyne or for anyone. You're not in the race, nothing matters any more. Well, so what? Not your concern, nothing to do with you. Just be so good as to sit down where you belong, at the piano.' But finally the threat to Lena jolts him out of his inertia and he accepts his new involvements and responsibilities. Because they undermine all this, the last scenes represent the triumph of mediocrity, of isolation, and of resignation.

The material, strictly speaking less auto-biographical than *Les Quatre Cents Coups,* is nonetheless a logical extension of the director's autobiography. It is not by accident that the gangsters, abducting Charlie and Lena, find themselves driving along behind a van advertising

Cahiers du Cinéma; that Charlie's brother is called Chico after one of the Marx brothers; or that Charlie himself should have been so called, because of Aznavour himself, but also because the character in the book was compared to Chaplin. Truffaut's well-known attitude to censorship gives point to Charlie's covering of Clarisse's breasts, because 'in films, that's how it has to be'. The censors took revenge by prohibiting the film to people under eighteen.

And if the sheet scene and probably the car-ride recall *A bout de souffle*, the ending in the snow is strongly reminiscent of the end of Lewis Seiler's *Big Shot,* with Humphrey Bogart, whom he had already written into the scenario of *A bout de souffle.* Even the phrase *rentrez chez vous, c'est un accident* 'was a key phrase for me: in almost

Tirez sur le pianiste: *Charlie at the heart of Parisian society: at the piano where he belongs (left) and with Clarisse (Michèle Mercier).*

every American film someone says it. That phrase had to go in there.'

One of the aspects of Truffaut's character we meet for the first time here is his taste for cabaret, with its typical songs, music, and dances. His knowledge of the Paris music-hall was second only to his knowledge of the cinema, and he visited cabarets and music-halls almost as regularly. Aznavour too, came from this background, and something of the atmosphere is recreated in the music he is given as well as in the night-club numbers. Philipe Repp and Henri Vigoureux, respectively the English-master and the night-watchman in *Les Quatre Cents Coups*, had come from the music-hall; so does Serge Davri, who plays Plyne; and of course the marvellous song *Ah! Vanille et framboise*, which Truffaut lovingly allows to be sung in full, was part of the singer's current cabaret act. Similarly, one of Truffaut's favourite songs by Félix Leclerc, 'Dialogue des amoureux', happens to be on the radio during the overnight car-journey, and helps to create a feeling of stillness and tranquillity at this point.

As before, the fact that people, incidents and settings are present because of their appeal to the author rather than for their value in the plot helps to create an atmosphere of unpredictability. Truffaut was pleased that he had not included a single scene of which the sole function was to render the plot more credible. On the other hand he included many which wilfully interrupt and sidetrack it. The stranger, Plyne's thoughts on women, Bobby Lapointe's song, all interrupt the story and remind us of Truffaut's interest in people whose mannerisms he is pleased to record. Even at the climax of the gangster story our attention is drawn away from the battle towards the touching death scene, and we never find out what happens to the loot: Truffaut lets the gangsters roar off, happy to be rid of them at last.

Shooting started on 30 November 1959 at Levallois on the outskirts of Paris, and finished in mid-January with the mountain scenes shot near Grenoble. At first, Truffaut thought of shooting the interiors in a studio, but found that they would cost three times the same sequences shot in natural settings. Probably the real reason was a fear of the unknown. Nervous of dealing with organisations, and conscious of his years of criticising the studio-made, quality tradition, he had, on the other hand, confidence gained through experience in his ability to use natural settings. Discussing Autant-Lara's claim that he couldn't work outside a studio, he says 'It's not true: he's afraid. Myself I say I don't like studios. In reality I'm scared stiff. We pretend. I'm scared; he's scared; we're all scared.'

Again, he used Dyaliscope and post-synchronised sound. Even with sound added later it is usual to record the background noises direct, which involves following the action with a microphone suspended just outside the frame, and the consequent danger of its silhouette or its shadow being recorded. Truffaut bitterly contrasted the perfection of photography with the primitive sound systems. In this case, however, a certain crudity in both was considered acceptable, as conveying an impression of documentary authenticity. He used two cameras (and later three) to record each take – one for general shots, the other hand-held by Raoul Coutard for close-ups. Truffaut wryly observed that the weight of the camera gave the operator a vested interest in getting the scene right first time. Multiple cameras make for fluent editing. Truffaut almost certainly used the system in imitation of Renoir who the previous year had made *Le Testament du Dr Cordelier* for TV (where multiple cameras are the norm) using as many as eight or ten cameras to record one scene.

Also from Renoir comes the tendency to modify the scenario drastically during shooting. The shooting script of this film gives only perfunctory stage-directions, which disappear after the first few pages, as does the script itself after scene 69, Charlie's arrival at the family hide-out. The last sixth of the scenario probably existed only on scraps of paper. Those directions that do exist include such phrases as 'Depending on how I feel on the day, Fido will appear at this point or not.' Nevertheless, the changes are not as radical as in *Les Quatre Cents Coups*: Truffaut now had a clearer view of the form he wanted the film to take.

Tirez sur le pianiste: *Charlie provoked too far, and without his piano, gets into a fight.*

As with all his films at this period, his first inclination seems to have been for an extensive commentary which would introduce the film and explain several purely visual scenes. The fragments that remain jar with the sections of internal monologue from Charlie, and later from Lena, and give an impression of inconsistency. The script began by casually introducing Charlie, then deserted him to relate Chico's arrival. The film version is therefore more inherently dramatic in building up characters. Truffaut seized any opportunity to push the film towards burlesque. The comic breakdown was originally simply a petrol stop, and the exaggerated shivering of the gangsters was probably spontaneous, since it was being shot in mid-winter. Equally, the autobio-

graphical aspects were strengthened during shooting by the last-minute addition of some of the timidity scenes, and also by all the indications of literary or cinematic taste. But most important, the original script had a long monologue in which Charlie pays homage to his old music-teacher. This section bears a strong resemblance to Truffaut's accounts of his own relationship with André Bazin. Clearly, when it came to shooting, this testimony, written so soon after Bazin's death, seemed unacceptable.

The flashback, the central section of the film, was much longer in the scenario, with memories within memories, soliloquies, and further commentaries. That he was rather self-conscious about this section is shown by the phrase appended to it: 'FLASHBACK (the first in my work, as yet somewhat insubstantial)'. Extensive cuts were made during shooting, but it is still unsatisfactory. Much better is the brief flashback in which Plyne is seen betraying Charlie. This was reduced to the time required for Ernest's description of it by dividing

Tirez sur le pianiste: Lena (Marie Dubois), Charlie and série noir *jalopy.*

it into three and having the end of each shot overlap with the beginning of the next.

Finished in January, the film was not shown to the French public until the end of the year. It met with a curious reception. Critics praised it highly, and almost unanimously, as better than *Les Quatre Cents Coups* and with *A bout de souffle* the most important film of the New Wave. Possibly forewarned that it was not conceived for the general public, but rather for the initiated, they were better predisposed towards it than it deserved. Despite this praise it was not a popular success, though the producer did not lose money on it. For Truffaut, however, 'of those who saw it, eight out of every ten walked away disappointed. So for me it was a failure. There's no point in wasting people's time.' This sensitivity to implied criticism

is as strong in him as it is in Charlie. He wants to combine the desire to express himself with the desire to entertain. When one critic remarked that he seemed to look on his films as a sort of circus spectacle, he was delighted: 'Precisely. My films are circus shows, and I'm glad of it. I never put on two elephant acts together. After the elephant, the juggler, and after the juggler, the bears. I even allow a sort of intermission towards the end of the sixth reel, because by then people's attention is flagging. At the seventh reel I take them in hand again, and try to end with a flourish . . . I swear I'm not joking: I think of the circus while working. I'd like to see people hiss and boo the unsuccessful sequences and clap those they liked. And since in order to see my films people have to shut themselves up in the dark, I never fail, towards the end of a film, to take them out into the countryside, beside the sea, or in the snow, so they'll forgive me . . . I've created certain laws for myself, often quite naïve, but they mean a lot to me and I try to improve them from film to film.

'If you like, it's a cinema of compromise in the sense that I think constantly of the public, but it's not a cinema of concessions, because I never use a comic effect I haven't myself laughed at, or a sad one that hasn't moved me. That said, I'm not completely satisfied with any of my films: there's always something important that didn't come off. It's very hard to bring off a really good circus show.'

was to consign him to several years out of favour. Godard's second film had just been banned, and the first films of Rivette and Rohmer, promised to the public for nearly two years, were still not available and proved disappointing when they did appear. For over a year, no New Wave film had been a commercial success and producers and public alike were beginning to lose faith in them. Truffaut admitted that he and his friends were going through a bad time, and attributed it to the

Tirez sur le pianiste: *Charlie's brothers Richard (J. J. Aslanian), Chico (Albert Rémy).*
Fido in the hands of Ernest (Daniel Boulanger).

Not only was the cool reception a severe blow to him, but it came at a crucial time for the group as a whole. Chabrol had attempted, in *A Double Tour,* to do something similar to *Pianiste,* but it had met with similar coolness. As well as dividing its characters evenly into 'beautiful' and evil ones, like *Tirez sur le pianiste, A Double Tour* had a similar symbolic subject underlying the murder mystery. Chabrol said that for him it depicted 'the massacre of beauty.' His *Les Bonnes Femmes* was proving equally unsuccessful, and *Les Godelureaux*

fact that, in attempting to emancipate themselves from the industry, they were making comparatively unsophisticated films on simple subjects. The qualities they aimed at – grace, lightness, elegance, discretion, rapidity – were dangerously close to the faults of frivolity, naïvety and superficiality.

If he was shaken by this criticism, there were others that he was confident were unjustified. Accused of mixing genres, he said the whole concept of genres was out of date; accused of producing a parody, and therefore a parasitic film, he protested that he detested parody: what had guided him was the concept of affectionate pastiche. In particular, he brushed aside the accusation that he and his friends were basing their films on minor social or personal problems in a world where bigger issues were at stake. Basically he was being called on to justify an apparent lack of political awareness at a time when France was involved in extremely violent post-colonial conflicts. He refused his critics any right to prescribe what films he should make; their job was simply to judge the ones he did make. 'When a journalist asks why we younger directors aren't making films about Algeria, I feel like replying "Why aren't you writing a book about Algeria? Because you wouldn't know what to write . . . Well, I wouldn't know what to film." The reality is too complex and foreign to me. I only film things I know thoroughly.' Not that politics didn't interest him: on the contrary, he consumed all books and films available on contemporary history, once called Resnais's *Nuit et brouillard* 'the greatest film ever made', and admired him enormously for being able to make such an influential gesture. But he himself was always too ready to see all sides of a question, too capable – like the pianist with Plyne – of understanding even the enemy's point of view, to be able to assert and persevere with one particular line. Rather than documentary or *cinéma vérité* he always preferred fiction, based on his own modest experience. 'This doesn't exclude ideas on life, the world, society. But I like anything that confuses the issue, that sows doubt; my bedside reading is 'La Séquestrée de Poitiers'; I only like unexpected details, that prove nothing; I like all that reveals the vulnerability of man . . . Why exalt workers, who hate what they're doing? During the period of my life when I was a welder, I would escape from my work by reconstituting mentally the three or four films I had seen the previous Sunday. And believe me, for nothing in the world would I have gone to see a film about workers.'

Despite his protestations, Truffaut's final feeling about the film seems to have been one of regret. By March 1961 he could say: 'Perhaps Chabrol shouldn't have made *A Double Tour* nor me *Le Pianiste*. These were detective novels we'd liked long before becoming established, and when you're in a position to realise an old dream you say "I'd certainly like to make that thing I read years ago."'

Tirez sur le pianiste: *Charlie and Lena: liebestod à la Truffaut.*

Tirez sur le pianiste: *Momo (Claude Mansard) the aggressor.*

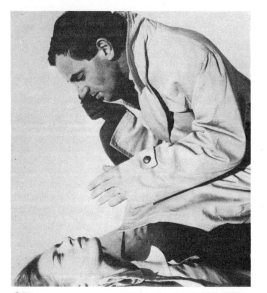

At the last minute you realise it wasn't worth the effort.' These mistakes were rendered all the more critical by the general context of uncertainty then prevailing in the French cinema. Attendances had fallen to their lowest level since the war, largely due to the spread of TV and the steady drop in the real value of workers' wages. People could no longer afford to go to films, especially when they were paying off hire purchase on a TV set which showed them five films a week. Producers who had never loved the younger directors, but only their sudden success, had been further hit when Malraux removed state aid to the industry on the grounds that other countries of the newly-formed Common Market didn't have it. It was imperative that the New Wave directors, and Truffaut in particular, should reassert their ability to combine the expression of their personal preoccupations with a wider popular appeal.

TRUFFAUT AND BAZIN

(a) *As in the scenario (cut from the film)*
CHARLIE: You see, if it hadn't been for Zélény, I'd never have become a pianist; he's the only bloke that ever helped me; he was a father to me; he not only taught me to play the piano, he taught me to be a man. He was a remarkable fellow, and I owe him everything worthwhile that ever happened to me; to speak to him was like bathing in the Ganges, for a Hindu. He was far from well, but his moral health was impressive. He borrowed money openly, and lent it discreetly. With him, everything became simple, clear and frank. When he went away for a few days, he always looked for a friend to lend his house to, and another to lend his car to.
TERESA: He must have loved you a lot.
CHARLIE: He loved everyone without exception; people are always asking, is the world just or unjust, but I'm certain that it's people like Zélény who make it better, because from believing life worthwhile and acting as if it was, he did good to all those that knew him; you could count on the fingers of your hand the people who wronged him. In his presence, in contact with him, astonished

by so much purity, it was impossible not to give him the best of oneself. His secret was goodness, and goodness is perhaps the secret of genius.
(b) *Truffaut's official memorial to him, published in Arts No. 697, 19 November 1958:*
André Bazin, who has just died at the age of 40, was the best writer on the cinema in Europe. Since the day in 1948 when he got me my first job connected with the cinema, working alongside him, I became his adoptive son, and thus owe him everything happy that ever happened to me thereafter.

He taught me to write on the cinema, correcting and publishing my first articles, and it's thanks to him that I managed to graduate to directing. He died a few hours after the first day's shooting of my film . . .

André Bazin was, like Giraudoux' characters, a man from 'before the days of original sin'. Everyone knew him to be honest and good, but his honesty and goodness always surprised one by their richness; to speak with him was like bathing in the Ganges, for a Hindu . . .

André's poor physical health was only equalled by his always astonishing moral health: he borrowed money openly and lent it discreetly: with him, everything became simple, clear and frank. As he considered it immoral to travel alone in a four-seater car, he would often stop at the Nogent bus-stop to give three commuters a lift into Paris; when he was away from home for a few weeks with his wife and little boy, he would see if there was, amongst his innumerable friends, someone in need of a house to whom he could lend his, and another to whom he could lend his car . . .

I don't know if the world is vicious or just, but I'm certain that it's people like Bazin who make it better, for, believing life worthwhile and acting as if it was, André did good to all those around him; and you could count on the fingers of one hand the number of people who wronged him; every single person who ever spoke to Bazin, though it be only once, can call himself his 'best friend', since in contact with him, overwhelmed by so much purity, it was impossible not to give him the best of oneself . . .

Jules et Jim

Tirez sur le pianiste was to be a film without a subject, 'to introduce into a detective story of little significance all that I wanted to say about glory, success, failure, frustration, women and love. It was a sort of hold-all that I tend to reject, now.' As a reaction, he felt the necessity to make a film in which the intrigue was not just a vehicle for the message, but was intimately linked to it: *Jules et Jim* exactly fitted.

It is adapted from the first novel of Henri-Pierre Roché who had published it at the age of seventy-four. Largely autobiographical, it deals with the period 1907–1930. Two years after its publication by Gallimard in 1953, Truffaut came across it by chance in a second-hand bookstall, in the Place du Palais Royal, and was immediately enthusiastic. He has gone so far as to say that 'reading it decided my vocation for the cinema'. Specifically, he decided that if ever he had the opportunity to make a film, this would be the first. As it happened, circumstances and economic arguments made *Les Quatre Cents Coups* his first feature, and subsequently he again postponed the delicate task of adapting a book so dependent on style, and based on such a potentially sensational situation. He had mentioned the book as matter for an excellent film in a critical review of Edgar Ulmer's *Naked Dawn* (1955), describing the characters as living in accordance with 'an original aesthetic morality, constantly reconsidered.' The review was communicated to Roché and pleased him greatly. He wrote to Truffaut, and in the course of the correspondence that followed he mentioned that he would be glad to see Truffaut turn to directing films, and was confident he would do justice to an adaptation of this particular book. On seeing *Les Mistons* he became even more confident, seeing in that film something of the atmosphere of his book.

When Jeanne Moreau joined Truffaut to make her brief appearance with Brialy in *Les Quatre Cents Coups,* he showed her the book. She recognised the possibilities in the female lead, and declared it the part she most wanted to play. Truffaut showed her photograph to Roché, who wrote back that she bore a striking resemblance to Catherine: 'I absolutely must meet her: bring her to me.' Five days later he died.

Truffaut had not however bought the rights to the book, and soon after that Gallimard began casting round to find a director or producer who might be interested. They tried Resnais and Godard. The producer Raoul Lévy thought it a

Jules et Jim: *Jim (Henri Serre), Catherine (Jeanne Moreau) and Jules (Oskar Werner).*

possibility, and himself suggested it to Jeanne Moreau, who protested, thinking Truffaut already had the rights. Truffaut refused to deal with Raoul Lévy, because he disapproved of his methods. Luckily, Truffaut had used some of the profits from his films to produce, amongst others, a beautiful little film on the sex-life of certain insects, for Roché's son, and was therefore on good terms with him. He got the rights and was able to make the film in complete freedom.

He had intended to start shooting in June 1960 a film called *Bleu d'outre-tombe,* based on a novel by René-Jean Clot, but renounced it in favour of *Jules et Jim.* It, too, was to have had Jeanne Moreau: disapproving of the tragic roles she was always given, Truffaut wanted to use her in a role where she could express gaiety and vitality. Now he chose to accompany her two actors less known to the French public: he went to Vienna to sign Oskar Werner, whom he had admired in Max Ophüls' *Lola Montès*; and after a long search found Henri Serre in a Left-bank theatre. Boris Bassiak came from his beloved music-hall, and Marie Dubois, who had played the female lead in *Tirez sur le pianiste,* was given a small (though originally larger) part. Denise, too – 'sex in its pure state' – had appeared briefly in the previous film as the violinist in the audition scene.

It's easy to see why Truffaut was so immediately attracted to the book. As well as the impressionistic presentation of the material in brief unconnected touches, he must have found in it all the elements of his own personal mythology. Jim is reputed to be the author's persona in the original story, but Truffaut identifies himself rather with Jules, and develops Oscar Werner's role in ways that recall both Antoine Doinel and Charlie. Jules inherits Charlie's timidity and general lack of assertiveness, particularly in his relationships with women. Jim helps Jules by passing his own cast-offs on to him, and Catherine remarks that what most fascinated her in Jules was his 'generosity, his innocence, his vulnerability'.

This timid, vulnerable man finds himself involved in two principal relationships which allow Truffaut to discuss those themes so dear to him: Love, Friendship, and Woman as an elusive

Jules et Jim: *Jules and Catherine with a new toy.*

idealised myth-figure. Other relationships which appeared in the book were removed for the sake of simplicity, although Truffaut incorporates fragments into the relationships between Catherine and the two men. Moreover, the relationships undergo continual subtle modification allowing Truffaut to concentrate on the people and to their complexities. Certainly most of the film is set in the *belle époque,* a period dear to Renoir and therefore to Truffaut, who had enthused about Jacques Becker's *Casque d'or* for its recreation of the period. But as with Becker, the period is of secondary importance and Truffaut has said that if he had realised beforehand how long it took to attach a false moustache or arrange a woman's hair in authentic 1910 style he would never have attempted it. For Roché had in fact given him permission to up-date it, and if he decided to leave it in the distant past it was solely with a view to preserving the atmosphere of gentle nostalgia that pervades the book.

He was, then, only interested in the relationships, together with the fact that they were at once violently unconventional and yet presented with a total innocence and simplicity. Always an individualist, he saw here a chance of upholding the right of the individual to recreate for himself the rules of conduct and to follow his own conscience rather than the dictates of society or religion.

Jules and Jim are both men of letters, and though their artistic attempts are not given much space in the film, we are allowed to hear an extract from a book Jim is writing based on his intense friendship for Jules. In the scenario these phrases were to have appeared in a formal introduction, and Jim's book was to have been about the other principal theme of the film, the existence somewhere in the world of an 'ideal woman' exactly suited to a given man; and conversely, the existence 'for each woman of a unique man, created for her, who is her intended husband'. Similarly, Gilberte was to have been identified with Eternity, and another, Lucie, with Absence – all clearly abstract, inhuman concepts. Thus the themes were to have been much more openly expressed than they are in the final version, and the association of the book Jim is writing with the film Truffaut was making much more obvious. Nevertheless Truffaut's 'cult of friendship' is so lyrically presented in visual terms that there is no need for it to be underlined

verbally. The two men are in a sense complementary, as the film implies in the comparison to Don Quixote and Sancho Panza. Their opposition is not only physical: one is French, the other German, and some effort is expended on establishing complementary characteristics deriving from their nationalities, in a manner reminiscent of Giraudoux, who, apart from being a favourite author of Truffaut, was an exact contemporary of Roché. Jim is 'direct' and, taking a general view, can see Catherine as a whole, whereas Jules, the specialist, concentrates on details. Jules is content to retire to the country, immersed in the natural sciences, while Jim is described by his teacher as *un curieux*, enquiring and restless.

Similarly, there can be no doubt of Catherine's symbolic function. She represents in Jules's mind

Jules et Jim: *Catherine resembling the antique statue.*

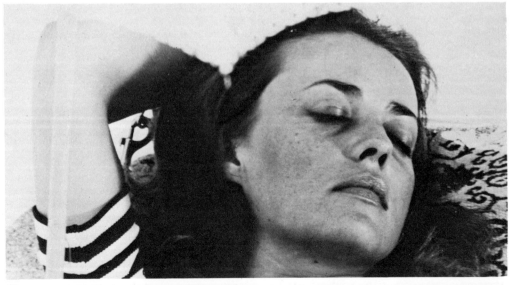

60

Woman, an apparition destined for all men, not a wife for one. Referred to as *Elle* in the scenario, she is a timeless concept, first glimpsed in Albert's photograph of an antique statue: a visionary goddess whose unreal and fugitive nature is echoed in the film by her wilful obscurities, her mystification, and the almost religious awe with which her men regard their initiation into her mysteries. Conscious of this image and of her responsibilities to it, she must dominate every situation, even if she has to cheat or deceive in order to do so. An absolute figure, she requires absolute commitment from those around her, and will not be content with compromises or shared loyalties. The pattern is remarkably similar to that underlying several of Renoir's films; he, too, delighted in building a film around a woman he admired, and presenting her with a choice between three contrasting men. Nora Grégor in *La Règle du jeu*, Anna Magnani in *Le Carrosse d'or* and Ingrid Bergman in *Eléna et les hommes*, each had to choose from among three men. In a sense, Truffaut has inverted the pattern of his previous film, where he showed Charlie involved in relationships with three different women. Catherine refuses to choose between her three men: she wants them all, all the time. As we have come to expect Truffaut shows this craving for the absolute as an inevitable prelude to despair and death. Towards the end, Jim comes dangerously close to appreciating Catherine objectively, seeing her activities as a game, a performance. Enraged at this ultimate betrayal, humiliated at being 'understood', afraid of seeing herself defined once and for all as merely relative, she tricks Jim into one final definitive relationship, death.

When the three of them are nearest to attaining their ideal equilibrium, the film takes us out into the countryside, and we are treated to lake, sky, and wide sweeps of forest. As at the end of *Les Quatre Cents Coups* and in the mountain scenes of *Tirez sur le pianiste*, a unity with nature serves as a formal sign for the highest attainable state of grace. Here they are 'nearest to heaven' as the commentary says and the photography communicates a sensation of liberation. The contrast is present in this film, too, though not so obviously.

Jules et Jim: *Alberte (Boris Bassiak) and Catherine.*

The city-scenes and human society, where the complications and constant meeting and parting represent the relative, are evoked in Bassiak's song 'La Tourbillon de la vie'.

Within this general outline, Truffaut here emphasises something he will return to again and again in later films: the impossibility of ordering Reality, or of defining rules of behaviour for all individuals and all situations. Truffaut echoed Renoir in saying that this film, if he brought it off, would be a hymn to love, and even a hymn to life; but unlike the films of Renoir this one proposes no simple clear-cut solutions to the problems of love and life. At all costs Truffaut preserves the inherent opaqueness and the infinite gradations and complexities of life, even at the cost of severely disconcerting his viewers. Rather than allow any one interpretation of the film to prevail, he deliberately set about confusing the issue, planting clues that suggest alternative solutions: 'As soon as one interpretation seems to be winning out, I destroy it, to avoid intellectual comfort, both for the spectator and for myself. I try to be objective, so I present a thousand different facets of reality. You must always try to see things from other people's points of view, because "everyone has his reasons" . . . To present these conflicting viewpoints and never offer a judgment on them can seem like a weakness. I see the danger, but think the artist must live with this paradox. For me, the man can and must judge. The artist, never.' This is what Truffaut means when he says he thinks of himself as a realist. One corollary of it is that all the characters must be regarded as having an equally valid view of events: the camera must not favour one character at the expense of the others, there must be no division of the characters into sympathetic and unsympathetic (he criticises Prévert's scenarios), or into star and minor roles. He was dissatisfied with *Les Quatre Cents Coups* principally because of this weakness: the children are too sympathetic, the adults too objectionable. As a result, his constant pre-occupation in *Jules et Jim* was to prevent Jeanne Moreau overshadowing the two men. However, Claude Mauriac expressed the criticism of most reviewers: 'Jeanne Moreau disturbs the equilibrium. She makes a film on friendship into a film on Love, and a *film d'auteur* into a *film de comédienne.'*

Summing up, Truffaut said that 'life must escape all the ideas that the spectator may have formulated about it. What may seem exceptional has to be made natural. One must dissuade the spectators from judging the characters. One must prevent them – and therefore oneself – from dominating the characters.' In this atmosphere of uncertainty, the only certainty is what to reject; for the rest, constant experimentation is proposed. The universe is seen as an inexhaustible field; everyone must establish his own code, and constantly reconsider that code in the light of further exploration; love itself must be reinvented anew by each lover. 'It's good to attempt to rediscover human laws . . . we have experimented with the very sources of life, and lost . . . I think like you

that in love the couple is not ideal. You only have to look around you. You wanted to build up something better, refusing hypocrisy and resignation; you wanted to invent love . . .' Catherine in the scenario says: 'We must begin again from nothing and rediscover the rules, willing to run any risk, and paying in cash.' One of Truffaut's friends, Pierre Kast, had recently said much the same thing in *La Morte Saison des amours,* where the couple is similarly rejected in favour of three- and four-sided relationships which prove 'natural' to the people concerned. While Kast's film ended on an optimistic note, for Truffaut these new relationships would prove just as unsatisfactory as the couple. 'I wanted people to be aware of the possibility of seeking other ethics, other ways of life, even knowing that all such arrangements would be doomed to failure.' What matters is the search, not the attainment; by analogy, what matters is that Truffaut should have posed the problem.

The themes of imperfect society and the need to reinvent love are combined in a rather curious secondary theme, most of the elements of which seem to have been added at the last moment, for they don't appear in the scenario. They perhaps developed from the scene of *'les trois fous'*, where the trio is presented as a group of grimacing outsiders, regarded with amused tolerance by the village, and by implication, like Antoine in *Les Quatre Cents Coups,* more whole and authentic than the society which rejects them. Godard does something similar in *Bande à part* and *Pierrot le fou.* This negation of social norms is picked up at several points by suggestions of homosexuality – not between Jules and Jim, though it is apparent that the villagers rather suspect that too, but amongst the men and their women. Gilberte and Albert, associated respectively with Jim and Catherine, recalling as they do the characters in Proust, suggest concealed homosexuality. Catherine early on adopts the guise of a man to stroll through the streets with Jules and Jim. After this, we can't be blamed for seeing more than a foreigner's mistake when Jules tells her *'Tu es fou'.* Later still, in another added scene, Jules points out the inversion of genders operating between

German and French for certain key words, including love. Last mentioned of these words is Life, neuter in German, which Jim admits to be more logical. There is something of this neuter 'middle role' in Catherine, who is seen as an incarnation of the life force. The commentary itself indicates that the men were touched by her masculine role 'as by a symbol that they couldn't quite understand'. One of Truffaut's friends defined it as 'that mythological fusion of the sexes for which we retain a certain nostalgia'. This links with Truffaut's nostalgia for a Paradise Lost, since it represents the same desire for a state of tranquillity, serenity and peace. This symbolic undertone to Catherine's role, involving the conciliation of opposite elements, comes out in the film in yet another way: her association with the conflicting elements of fire and water. One or other of these figures prominently in every decisive step of her life: water, in the plunge into the river; fire, when she expurgates her past in the form of the letters; rain helps her to decide on the trip to the coast, and later decides her return to Paris. Water is the death she chooses for herself and for Jim, and their coffins are consumed by fire. It is not by accident that she always took with her a bottle of vitriol, 'liquid fire'.

Jules et Jim: *Catherine and her child Sabine (Sabine Haudepin) and with Jules and Jim in the fatal car.*

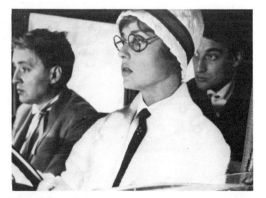

Finally, all that Catherine stands for is assured a continuity in spite of her death. Sabine represents the assimilation of two daughters in the book into a single girl. She is shown repeating various gestures of Catherine, such as knitting in the corner, or pinching the bridge of her nose when she takes off the glasses. She is at once a future Catherine and a substitute for the present one. When one of the men is seeking Catherine's favour, he courts Sabine; when rejected by Catherine, he turns to Sabine as a sort of consolation.

Any director espousing an unconventional point of view must face the problem of making his message palatable. 'It's not a question of concessions, nor of saying "That's too strong for them, I'll leave it out"; it's a question of doing what you want to, but reflecting constantly on the best means of imposing it. I see this as a supplementary discipline.'

His solution in this case was to adopt a matter-of-fact, dispassionate tone – to present the potentially sensational and emotional material coolly so that the spectator would not feel he was being bullied into accepting something against his better judgment. This corresponds to Renoir's formula – the more emotional the material, the less emotional the treatment – and results, here, in a deliberately neutral mood recalling the films of Bresson. There is no extrovert display of emotion, no dramatic climax, no suspense. In all delicate scenes the actors are comparatively expressionless, and speak in flat unemotional voices. The post-synchronisation helped to eliminate any spontaneous emotion that might have crept into the dialogue during shooting.

Truffaut further discouraged any unfavourable reactions in the audience by bombarding them with impressions. The public are childish where physical love is concerned: certain lines of dialogue run an obvious risk of arousing embarrassed laughter, so the reply must break in quickly; similarly, certain things would arouse laughter if said in bed, for instance, and if the commentary becomes delicate I cut to an exterior shot of the chalet as seen from a helicopter, so that the sheer beauty of the countryside blocks the laughter in the spectator's throat.' The emotional nature of the material becomes less intense when reported indirectly in the commentary. This is taken straight from the book, and is spoken by Michel Subor in a neutral tone, very rapidly and without intonation. Bresson uses commentary for a similar purpose; Truffaut did not use it to such an extent again until *L'Enfant Sauvage* which, of all his other films, most resembles this in mood.

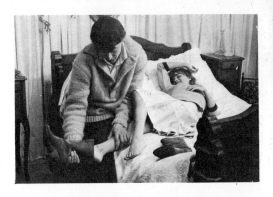

Jules et Jim: *Catherine obeys the dictates of her fancy and succumbs to the charms of Jim.*

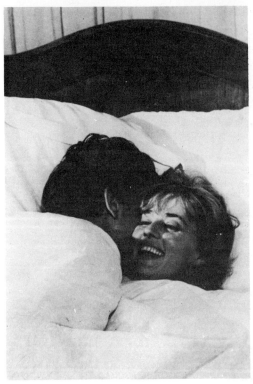

The discretion of the music is equally deliberate. Georges Delerue was overwhelmed when he saw the film, and suggested grandiose music to fit the subject. Truffaut insisted to the contrary. Similarly, with Coutard he sought an unemphatic camera style. The result would, he hoped, parallel the 'invisible style' which he so admired in the book itself. Another director might have seized this opportunity to mount a violent attack on 'our hypocritical authoritarian society'. But, for Truffaut, understatement is always preferable to overstatement: 'I believe in the modesty of appearances, even if it might with justice be called "false modesty". I am very fond of false modesty.'

Modestly, he always asked five or six trustworthy friends to read the scenario beforehand – preferably ones who intended to become directors, because they were more severe. When shooting was finished, he would show the rushes to another friend (Rivette in the case of Le Pianiste, Aurel with Jules et Jim). And get detailed advice. After the editing, he would spy on the technicians as they watched the film in its provisional form, noting any remarks made by the sound engineer, the projectionist, the composer or the recording engineer. 'In short I'm very open to influence, and not ashamed of it . . . Basically, I'm almost ashamed to be making films at all . . . It's such a mobilisation of capital and an immobilisation of personnel . . . the only way to give a sense to all this activity is to regard it as a spectacle, and one that must succeed. I've the impression (stupid, I know, since the make-up girls and dressers are paid the same whether the film's a success or not) that I'd be ashamed to meet them three months later if the film had flopped. I'd have the feeling of having dragged them into a pointless exercise, of having wasted two months of their life.'

In this film, his self-effacement extends to following the book in the majority of scenes. As well as assuring a greater degree of fidelity to the book's style, this system permitted him to avoid the methods of adaptation he had so strongly criticised in Aurenche and Bost. Instead, he chose as his model Jean-Pierre Melville's adaptation of Cocteau's 'Les Enfants Terribles'. This consisted of alternating scenes which have dialogue in formal theatrical style with other narrative sections accompanied by a commentary. At all costs he wanted to avoid the impression of a string of 'set pieces'.

Occasionally he did invent a whole scene, such as Catherine's furious defence of French wine, but only when he was sure it was in harmony with the rest and would not look like the intrusion of a foreign personality. He even controlled his characteristic inclination to call a sudden halt in the action while one of his characters meditates on something apparently irrelevant. The only time it happens is when Jim recalls an unnamed soldier (in fact Guillaume Appollinaire) who managed to wage his own private combat and assert his own private values within the context of the collective madness of World War I. This is clearly another variation on the theme of the conflict between the individual and collectivity. The fact that this story should have been included despite its relative dullness (the camera remains motionless for three long minutes while he tells it) is sufficient indication of the importance Truffaut attributes to the faintest echoes of the theme. The related question of collective inhumanity was stressed through considerable expansion of the war scenes. He had the previous year encouraged, produced, supervised, and acted a small part in the first film made by his friend Claude de Givray, about his recently completed military service. De Givray, who speaks of Truffaut much as Truffaut speaks of Bazin, had up-dated the play Tire au flanc, on which Renoir had also based an anti-war film in 1928. The result is that in Jules et Jim the war sequences, dismissed in a few lines in the book, have been expanded. An incidental result is that Truffaut was able to incorporate some impressive documentary shots. When asked why he had stretched some of these to CinemaScope width while leaving others in standard format, he pointed out that those with people in them would have looked grotesque and unreal on a wide screen, whereas the distorted tanks and explosions 'all of a sudden reveal war as frankly monstrous, which is logical'.

The film contains fewer asides, in-jokes, and other personal notations not directly connected with the central theme than do his previous films:

there is an obscure reference to a cat called Judex, which he couldn't bring himself to cut, and the rather self-conscious enunciation of the phrase *'le jour se lève'*. Catherine dressed up as a man bears a striking resemblance to the Kid, in Chaplin's film, and is called Thomas, after *Thomas l'imposteur*. There are two short extracts from films, one showing the burning of books, foreshadowing *Fahrenheit 451*; the other is a nondescript replacement for *Charlot soldat*, which

Jules et Jim: *Catherine, Jules and Jim and early Picasso.*

Truffaut had wanted to use both as homage to Chaplin and because of its relevance to the theme. The Picasso prints which appear in the background of several scenes had a different purpose. The book covers a period of some twenty-five years, from 1907 to about 1930. Even the film must logically extend over about fifteen years. Yet because Truffaut thought that ageing actors with make-up was ridiculous, we are not shown any signs of the passage of time in the appearance of the stars, or even of the child. Jean Gruault came up with the idea of using prints from the relevant periods of Picasso's artistic development. The result is a logical inconsistency, though Truffaut was completely satisfied.

On the other hand, he was not so pleased with the freeze-frames used during Catherine's grimaces and the friends' reunion. These, like the imprinting of Jules' *Pas celle-là* on the image, were probably used for emphasis within the context of an unemphatic style. Later, Truffaut considered the effect too obvious, and experimented with briefer and briefer 'stopping' of the images, until in *La Peau Douce* he uses images stopped for only 8 frames (one-third of a second) instead of the 35 frames (one-and-a-half seconds) used here. The result was almost subliminal.

The film was shot between 10 April and 3 June 1961, around Paris, in Alsace, and near St Paul de Vence on the Côte d'Azur. As usual, changes were made in the translation of the script into film, but they concerned form rather than theme. The order and length of the scenes were changed so as to condense, simplify and smooth out the development of the plot. The aerial views were a last-minute addition, and several scenes with erotic overtones have disappeared, whether from censorship or self-censorship is hard to say. Catherine was to make some suggestive remarks to Jules about her sexual practices with Jim, and at one point we were to see her in bed between Jim and Albert, with each wondering what the other is up to.

Something Truffaut first tried in this film which was later to become standard, was the introduction wherever possible of gently amusing scenes intended to combat the unforeseen melancholy of his earlier films. Here we see Jim greeting acquaintances, while Thérèse's autobiography flows implacably on; then there is the little man who alone can satisfy her; there is Denise – 'sex in its pure state', – and there is the hunt for the last signs of civilisation. Instead of improvising them as here, Truffaut was deliberately to base the whole of his later autobiographical films on such material, confident that the tragic element would insinuate itself, thus resulting in the desired balance of the two.

The première took place on 27 January 1962, and Truffaut was so nervous that instead of attending it he retreated to a Marx Brothers film. He needn't have worried: the critics were immediately and almost unanimously favourable, and the public supported this judgment. Only the censors protested, limiting attendance to people over 18. Truffaut pointed out that it couldn't be the adulterous aspects they objected to, since eight out of every ten films are based on these; what annoyed them was the lack of hypocrisy in the treatment, and the genuine objectivity with which the problems were discussed. It could, therefore, be considered a *censure à la qualité,* and as such most flattering.

He attributed the success to his having had the good fortune to recognise, as in *Les Quatre Cents Coups,* a potentially powerful subject which had never before been adequately treated in the cinema. Unlike *Tirez sur le pianiste,* this central theme had been intrinsically linked to the plot, and sufficiently strong to resist the debilitating effects which he admits his techniques have on a film in the course of shooting. Yet in very concrete ways this film represents a synthesis of all his previous films, including *Les Mistons* and *Tirez sur le pianiste.* It has in common with *Les Mistons* the Woman theme, the literary commentary, and a feeling for the outdoors – a 'sunny feel', Truffaut calls it. In common with *Les Quatre Cents Coups* it portrays a socially reprehensible creature with whom we are forced to sympathise. The central theme of both is the opposition between the indivi-.dual and the collective. As in *Tirez sur le pianiste* Truffaut insists on 'mixed characters' who are prey to conflicting impulses, indefinable and unpredictable. Like that. film it also consists of a series of variations on the theme of Woman and Love. Summarising his development, Truffaut says: 'In *Les Quatre Cents Coups* the subject was so important that the film itself faded into the background . . . But I had a strong. inclination also to play around with formal techniques, and this I stated in *Tirez sur le pianiste.* In this sense *Jules et Jim* is a synthesis: at once the great subject which carries you away and which you don't regret having chosen, and a project which inspires ideas at once formal and moral, visual and intellectual.'

L'Amour à vingt ans

During 1961 Pierre Rostang had proposed to Truffaut a film consisting of five sketches, to be shot by young directors of five different nationalities, on the topic of First Love. Truffaut immediately saw in it the chance to extend his own and Léaud's biography, by presenting Antoine's first romantic encounter. He could thus salvage an incident which he had planned to build into a feature, until Julien Duvivier's *Boulevard* (1960) made the project less attractive. Truffaut's agreement justified the undertaking in the producer's eyes, and the four other directors were chosen. Truffaut's influence can be measured by the choice of the sons of two of his favourite directors: Marcel, son of Max Ophüls, and Renzo, son of Roberto Rossellini. Unfortunately these two produced the least interesting of the resulting sketches. To link the five together, a song composed by Georges Delerue was to be sung in

L'Amour à vingt ans: Colette, Antoine and Colette's father and mother (François Darbon and Rosy Varte).

L'Amour à vingt ans: Antoine (Jean-Pierre Léaud) and Colette (Marie-France Pisier).

the relevant language in each episode; photographs arranged by Henri Cartier-Bresson would provide a further link. Inevitably, Léaud would play the lead, and to find a partner for him Truffaut published an advertisement. Out of some three hundred applicants, he chose Marie-France Pisier. Shooting began on 25 October 1961, before the première of *Jules et Jim*.

When asked beforehand what tone he intended to adopt in this sketch, Truffaut replied 'light and humorous: very similar to that of *Les Quatres Cents Coups,* at least in its lighter moments.' Experience should have warned him what would be likely to occur if he attempted to build another film solely around his adolescence. His first had become progressively gloomy in the course of shooting, and the same was to happen here. Speaking for all the directors, Truffaut said: 'We realised that it added up to a melancholy,

69

sometimes even desperate film, not because we had sought it but simply because love at twenty is inevitably somewhat sad, given the discrepancy between one's taste for the absolute – still acute at that age – and the pitiful compromises that go to make up adult life.'

Once again, then, the central theme is the pursuit of an ideal happiness, which had underlain all his previous films. In *L'Amour à vingt ans* it is first glimpsed during a Youth Concert, and the girl Antoine meets there is intimately associated with his appreciation of music. In *Jules et Jim* the association was with an antique statue. In either case, this ideal world contrasts sharply for Antoine, with the routine of existence. And just as Jules had been convinced that 'for every man there exists a woman meant for him', so Antoine can assure Colette 'anyway, we would have been certain to meet one day or another'. It is easy to foresee that such illusions will once again receive harsh treatment at Truffaut's hands. Obsessed with the image he has built up for himself, Antoine acts foolishly and romantically, and the girl, not prepared to respond on that level, finds him over-insistent and jealous. The reality is underlined by the sound of flushing when a girl goes to the lavatory next door. Many years will pass before Antoine is capable of accepting that young girls are only human.

He is left watching television with her parents – a poor consolation, but not quite as bad as it might seem, for Colette's mother and step-father are infinitely more understanding than Antoine's. They represent, in fact, the security that Antoine, rejected since his birth, has always sought. Nevertheless we are left with the impression of illusions shattered, of a gauche and not always admirable individual whose impulsive expression of a fiercely romantic imagination frightens away the people he wants to attract. Antoine is invariably too nervous to confess his admiration in person. He prefers to send his declaration by post (as he will again in *Baisers Volés*) or telegraph (like Pierre in *La Peau Douce*) or perhaps to say it with flowers.

Other autobiographical material is recognisable in the Clichy setting, the job as storeman, the

L'Amour à vingt ans: *Antoine bored to tears in the record store (above) and watching the Movietone News with Colette (below).*

reference to Maurice le Roux who had done the music for *Les Mistons*, and of course in the passion for the cinema which comes out here as a devotion to classical music, just as the Cinémathèque will become in *Baisers Volés* the Conservatoire. There was originally to be a sly dig, which regrettably never reached the final version of the film, at the founder of Les Films de la Pléiade: Antoine was not originally to work with Phillips, but with an imaginary music pub-

lisher, 'Les Editions du Carrosse, which enjoys a high reputation with music lovers, and which has taken over Les Editions de la Pléiade, wound up for fraud.' The transposition of Truffaut's cinematic preoccupations into the musical world is unexpected, because Truffaut himself has little appreciation of music as such. It is partly due to the fact that the role of Antoine includes elements of Léaud as well, whose interest in music extends to playing the piano. Incidentally it allows Truffaut to incorporate snatches of songs during the packaging scene, including one sung by Jeanne Moreau.

When Antoine and Colette visit the cinema, all we see is a Movietone News. On the other hand we do get a reference to Antoine's past experience in a fragment from *Les Quatre Cents Coups*. But the extract, introduced brusquely and almost inaudibly, is disconcertingly irrelevant even if one recognises it, incomprehensible if one doesn't. There is an enigmatic sequence in the dark auditorium where the two first meet. Truffaut was trying to create a counterpoint between music and image: 'I wanted the scene to advance along with the music. You couldn't know at what moment the public was going to notice the girl. To achieve a certain intensity, the camera isolates these two more and more as the scene progresses.

It's a long scene, and the interest is there, for me, in the interplay of music and action.'

Truffaut's sketch was finished by the end of 1961, but the complete series didn't receive its première until June the following year, when it opened the Berlin Film Festival and appeared simultaneously in Paris. Most critics were favourable, a surprising number going so far as to say it was his best work yet, and the first-night audience gave Truffaut's sketch in particular a long ovation. Certainly, however, it is fragmentary; and *La Peau Douce* took that aspect of the film a step further. Both films attempt to analyse a myth and show that reality is more complex than it usually seems in films. They are deliberately unromantic treatments of, in one case, adolescent love and, in the other, adulterous; in both there is the risk of a drab or sordid result. This was particularly acute with *L'Amour à vingt ans* because of the personal nature of the material and the emotional significance it had for Truffaut. He felt that, like *Jules et Jim*, it called for severe understatement, and used a similar neutral commentary to tone it down. Unfortunately, the material is not so intrinsically powerful as it seemed to him and the understatement only serves to detract further from any impact it might have had.

La Peau Douce

While he was in the United States to promote *Jules et Jim,* Truffaut had met Ray Bradbury and bought the rights of *Fahrenheit 451,* which he hoped to make during 1962. The scenario, however, took a long time to prepare, and three different versions were written. The film was to be in colour, production costs would be high, and the rights had been expensive. Truffaut could not afford to produce it himself, and the anti-social implications frightened off all potential French backers.

He had been working on the script with Jean-Louis Richard, to whom Jeanne Moreau had introduced him at a private projection of *Les Quatre Cents Coups,* and with whom he shared memories of military service. As an actor with Louis Jouvet in 1948, Richard had helped Jeanne Moreau get a chance to prove herself, and subsequently married her. Towards the end of 1962 she felt she would like to act in an

La Peau Douce: *Franca (Nelly Benedetti) and Pierre Lachenay (Jean Desailly).*

adventure film directed by Richard, so he and Truffaut retired to Cannes and wrote the script of *Mata Hari, Agent Secret H21.* With no possibility of shooting *Fahrenheit 451* before 1964, Truffaut decided to prepare the scenario for another film, to be shot on location, in black and white and within his own commercial reach. On August 1963, the two men once more retired to Cannes. By the simple expedient of tossing a coin, it was decided that Truffaut should direct this one.

It was to be about adultery. Truffaut describes the experience behind this decision: 'Years before, I had seen, or rather imagined, this image of a couple in a taxi. As I imagined it, the time was about 7.30 p.m.; they must be going home to dine, and they're not married, or if they are it's not to each other and each has several children of his own. It's a terribly sensual kiss in a taxi in a big city. When an image like that comes into your head, you tell yourself deep down "Even a subject like adultery has never been properly treated", and you feel as if you're going to say lots of new things: and it all started from there. And also from a sound, for I imagined that when they kissed their teeth clashed together.' Obviously, after that, the film had to be made.

Without suggesting the extent to which the film is autobiographical, it is apparent that *La Peau Douce* describes a similar experience to the autobiographical *Domicile Conjugal.* Moreover, like *Les Quatre Cents Coups, L'Amour à vingt ans,* and *Baisers Volés,* it is not an adaptation but an original scenario based solely on material from his own or his friends' experience, or culled from newspaper reports of actual incidents. He keeps a permanent dossier of newspaper cuttings, as a sort of document on human nature and human relationships, and they frequently serve as incidental material for his films. *La Peau Douce* includes elements of several such cases, including the Jaccoud affair in Geneva. In particular, French newspapers had reported Nicole Gérard's shooting of her husband in a restaurant in the Rue de la Huchette in 1963. Truffaut seized on this act of violence to solve the problem of ending the film, which had been giving him a lot of trouble. Perhaps it solves the problem too well, since it brushes

aside the complexities of the situation which it has been the purpose of the film to present, but he was glad to make use of it because he was afraid of producing another film in which, as in *L'Amour à vingt ans,* 'nothing whatsoever happens'. Yet to invent such an ending for purely formal purposes would be impossible to him. It is precisely because he is so fascinated by the extraordinary that he is so often led to adapt other people's stories. 'Whenever I know that a rare fact has actually happened, or if I come across it written down by someone else, then I can believe in it and adopt it as my own.' However, he included in the scenario several incidents destined to prepare the spectator for the final murder: the film was to begin with a suicide in the Metro, there was talk of a jet-plane exploding, we were shown the rifle early on, and while handling it the characters talked of hunting. All this was cut out in the editing, and now the violence is an isolated incident and can seem incongruous.

Truffaut was intent on destroying the conventional treatment of adultery. Few films had concentrated on presenting faithfully the practical difficulties and the anguish involved in an adulterous affair. This was one thing he had

La Peau Douce*: Franca, Pierre and the seeds of infidelity.*

admired in Autant-Lara's *En cas de malheur,* but he considered that one had otherwise to go right back to *Brief Encounter* to find the subject treated seriously. In a sense, Truffaut's own *Jules et Jim* had been a film on adultery, but only incidentally: the centre of interest had been a discussion of love and friendship. The triangular relationships had been based on sympathy and shared ideals, and the overwhelming impression is of ease and grace. No social or moral conventions interfere with the developing affections, and no practical contingencies (such as poverty, embarrassing misunderstandings, awkward lies or the fear of discovery) complicate the flow of the film. The total absence of these sordid aspects had somewhat undermined the moral of the film, that though current social and sexual mores are unsatisfactory, any new types of relationship will be equally disappointing. He wanted, therefore, in *La Peau Douce* to analyse precisely these petty complications which hinder the realisation of ideals. 'Current moral attitudes are unsatisfactory but I can't bring myself to believe in any others, for all the examples one sees around one are disastrous. Nothing ever works perfectly, at any level of society, and that's because of the way people are, not because of social, religious or political conditions.'

The three characters who form the triangle are Pierre (44), Franca his wife (38), and Nicole (22). Pierre is 'happily married', and yet becomes involved in an affair with a girl half his age. Basically, he is given a choice between the known and the unknown, between the routine compromises of living together and the romantic ideal of something better, that has survived as a relic of adolescent dreams. For, faced with the same violent irrational desire that Antoine had felt for Colette in *L'Amour à vingt ans,* Pierre acts in the same gauche way. The script specifically describes his behaviour as 'childish'. for instance when he fondles Nicole under cover of the tray of sweets. Childhood is the age of purity and absolute ideals for Truffaut. And like Antoine, of whom he could easily be an older version, Pierre misjudges the situation and frightens off the girl. She withdraws apologetically

La Peau Douce: *Nicole (Françoise Dorléac) and Franca thinking of themselves.*

leaving him alone in the half-built apartment, just as Antoine had been left resignedly watching television with Colette's parents. And finally, death will intervene as it had in *Les Mistons,* in *Tirez sur le pianiste,* and in *Jules et Jim,* to put an end to these illusions. The consistency in the thematic material of all these films is only equalled by the diversity of their external trappings: the conflict of the real and the ideal through the medium first of a gangster film, then of a period evocation, now of a sordid contemporary drama.

Following his assertion that everyone's reality is equally valid, Truffaut was constantly preoccupied during shooting with building up the wife's role as he had built up that of Jules. It would be facile to present an unsympathetic wife, from whom Pierre naturally seeks refuge with a more attractive woman. The whole point of the film is that it is *ridiculous* for Pierre even to think of leaving his wife. She is much more passionate, sensual and 'real' than Nicole, whose weaker acting and conventional good looks combine to make her seem superficial. The fact that he does, however, desert his wife for her indicates the extent to which Pierre has lost control of his own life and actions.

As in Truffaut's previous films, the locations are associated with various aspects of the themes, just as are the characters. The trip to Lisbon represents an escape from reality, and the Ideal World is close to being realised: Nicole falls into Pierre's arms, and there are no petty complications. In an incident in the original scenario directly parallel to the Reims episode, Pierre was at this point to be momentarily embarrassed when the conference organiser caught him out in his lie about leaving the next morning, and this was to interfere with his first appointment with Nicole. This incident was cut, presumably to

Peau Douce: *(above) Nicole, airlines and bras: untouchable consumer society.*

Peau Douce: *(below) Nicole keeps Pierre out of focus.*

preserve this total identification between Lisbon, Nicole, and the exhilaration of the exotic. It is only early in the film that this ultimate happiness seems within reach. Subsequently, in the Paris episode, reality takes over and awkward problems arise. For Pierre, as for Charlie in *Tirez sur le pianiste*, 'It's Paris that's lousy for us'. The many practical difficulties culminate in the scene where he and Nicole are told they can have a room in a quarter of an hour. What had seemed beyond value is rapidly being cheapened.

Pierre arranges the two days in Reims in an attempt to recapture the easy *entente* of the Lisbon period; but this time, it is not enough to leave Paris. The complications multiply, both are feeling humiliated, and Pierre in a state of near-panic gets involved in a ludicrous series of lies to his friend. In a last desperate attempt to prove that the happiness he had envisaged is possible, Pierre takes Nicole to the country, which had represented to Antoine, Charlie and Jules both liberation and an ultimate reconciliation with life. The name of the hotel, La Colinière, is a sort of fetish, for it recalls the château in Renior's *La Règle du jeu*. Here all things again seem possible, but in fact the outcome will be as tragic as it was in Renoir's film. The return to Paris is an admission of defeat in itself, an admission that the influences of the countryside are powerless to combat the realities of despair and disillusion. *La Peau Douce* is the most definitively pessimistic of all Truffaut's films.

It is, in every sense, a realistic film, aimed at undermining myths and absolutes which, seductive as they may seem, spread disaster and despair if allowed to guide our actions. The cinema itself is under attack as chief disseminator of these myths, here opposed by an austere realism such as Truffaut had first tried to create in *L'Amour à vingt ans*. Pierre as a celebrated writer and Nicole, an air-hostess, embody two modern myth-figures, and the film sets out to demystify these occupations, revealing fallible, confused individuals.

Pierre's nervousness is patently inherited from Antoine and Charlie, but, in him, timidity extends further towards vacillation and immaturity. It is certainly the cruellest self-portrait Truffaut has given us, the harshest judgment he could pass on his own weaknesses. His family resemblance to Antoine includes a similar inability to declare himself verbally to the woman he loves, a curious attribute in a professional talker. He can be splendidly passionate in a telegram, in a way reminiscent of Antoine's written declarations, and in a scene edited out of *La Peau Douce* he was to fall back on flowers to express his affection. To underline the link between the two men, the original scenario indicates that Nicole's brother is called Antoine and that he is nineteen years old – two years older than the Antoine of *L'Amour à vingt ans,* which was shot two years earlier. Other material edited out of the final film mentions that this Antoine is engaged to marry a girl called Colette.

Antoine and Charlie expressed Truffaut's interest in the cinema as an interest in music; Pierre displays a similar enthusiasm for literature. The analogy is the neater for Pierre's literary

La Peau Douce: *Nicole keeps her youth.*

career being linked with the cinema through the film on Gide he presents at Reims. Truffaut had of course been presenting his own and other people's films in just such a way for years. The relevance of Gide's lines in 'La Séquestrée de Poitiers' is self-evident: 'I bring no doctrine, I refuse to give advice, and in an argument I immediately back down. But I know that today many are feeling their way tentatively, not knowing what to put their trust in. To them I say: Believe those who seek the truth, doubt those that find it, doubt everything, but don't doubt yourself.' This is one aspect of Pierre's lack of self-assertion that is defined as a strength and not a weakness. The presence of Frank in the film is intended to provide a point of comparison. As Pierre says of him, '. . . you know, Frank, I don't know him, but just like that, from his manner, he represents everything I detest in the world . . . the bloke who's sure of himself, who doesn't give a damn . . .'

This is Truffaut's latest portrait of himself: publicly successful but privately vulnerable, and diffident to the point of indecision; this latter quality being sometimes valuable, more often harmful – particularly when it allows his actions to be guided by out-dated romantic dreams. Pierre is a logical extension of Antoine, Charlie and Jules, but not a complete self-portrait in that Truffaut himself is sufficiently aware of his temptations to try to exorcise them in this cruel analysis.

The film was begun on 21 October 1963, and shot in Lisbon, Reims and near Paris. Because Jean Desailly was acting at the Odéon each evening, the locations were adapted as far as possible to his convenience, and many of the office scenes were filmed in the offices of the Théâtre de France. All the leading actors were chosen before the scenario was written, so that the plot could be built around their personalities. Truffaut chose three professional actors because he felt that the film's dependence on subtleties and overtones called for the experience of professionals.

The scenario was designed to consist of a large number of extremely brief takes, unlike most other scripts at the time. The average number of takes in a film is about 500: Godard had been making films of only 250 or 300, and in *Vivre sa Vie* these had been further grouped into as few as twelve tableaux. *La Peau Douce* consists of about 800 takes. 'Lately there've been too many takes of a minute's duration or more. I've seen a lot of films these last few years where it seemed to me that with 120 more takes they would have been a success. It all goes too quickly, it's too schematic, the situations aren't analysed enough . . . Quite aside from the technical skill necessary to bring off longer sequences, certain scenes and situations need to be cut up more.' The choice of

a standard screen rather than the wide screen Truffaut had used exclusively up to this point means that the action is constantly moving out of this restricted field of view, necessitating repeated changes of angle. Consequently the action is broken up, and individual movements and objects are isolated for our attention. With *Jules et Jim*, 'it had constantly been necessary to integrate nature and the environment into the narrative, hence all those 360° pans. On the other hand, as *La Peau*

La Peau Douce: *the bedroom at La Colinière Hotel.*

Douce is surgical in nature, the camera must on no account pan: it hadn't the right to go off for a casual stroll. The critics said I'd changed my style; not at all, I'd merely changed my subject.' There is a danger that the emotional continuity will be lost when a scene is fragmented. To avoid this, Truffaut had some scenes played straight through, but filmed with at least two cameras. By editing the different versions, he could combine the required brevity of take with an overall continuity.

The final film differs very little from the original scenario, probably because both writing and shooting took place so quickly. The Lisbon episode was to have taken place in Milan. The daughter was to have been a son, but Truffaut used the girl from *Jules et Jim* instead. Several scenes were edited out to bring an already long film down to more acceptable commercial length. But the only major scenes rejected occur near the end of the film; probably they were cut to tighten the narrative as it approached its climax. It may also be that Truffaut was simply becoming exhausted by the very severity of the film. He has often explained how he needs a certain sympathy with the central characters; by contrast, of the progress of this film he said: 'I suffered after and even during shooting from the harsher side of it. It has the least feeling of all my films . . . It was a sort of autopsy, or drought, and I found myself unable to introduce into it the warmth I wanted. I had to be cold, and when you begin a thing you must keep at it. The worst possible thing that can happen to a director is to change horses in mid-stream. That is unpardonable. I kept at it right to the end, but I suffered from these characters for whom I didn't feel much affection, but who were there and couldn't be removed.'

His determination not to be side-tracked resulted in a film which resembles *Les Quatre Cents Coups*, and contrasts with the intervening two, in its cohesiveness and lack of digression. If he had always avoided the traditional 'set pieces', he had nevertheless included in *Jules et Jim* and in *Tirez sur le pianiste* musical 'items', or scenes depending on personal whim. With *La Peau Douce* he was again working solely with his own material, and didn't have to introduce his own personality and preoccupations into someone else's narrative. The resulting austerity disappointed most critics and the public, accustomed by his previous films to a more genial and wayward personality.

It is a fact that certain personal notations are present, but very discreetly, like La Coliniére, or the poster for Cocteau's *Le Testament d'Orphée*, which Truffaut had helped to finance with money earned from *Les Quatre Cents Coups*. Likewise, Truffaut mentions Sacha Guitry, or makes an off-hand reference to the crisis in the cinema; the phrase 'the first time I saw the sea was in a Paramount film', echoes Truffaut's own indifference to nature unless it is on the screen. In particular, there is Nicole's room number, 813, the title of one of Maurice Leblanc's Arsène Lupin novels that had been a great favourite in his childhood. In a short scene edited out, it was coincidentally to have been her flight number, and Pierre was to try unsuccessfully to buy her the book. None of the extant scenes depend for their existence on such information, external to the film's themes.

The film was selected for the Cannes festival of 1964, at which *Les Parapluies de Cherbourg* took the main prize. It opened in Paris on 20 May at no less than six cinemas, but received a mixed reception and seems to have disappointed most people. One critic described the film as 'a documentary on the gear changes of the Citroen'. Certainly, for a director whose dominant interest is individuals and their relationships, Truffaut had produced a film surprisingly cluttered with objects. There are close-ups of door-handles, keys, gear-levers, aeroplane instrument panels, and doors, radio buttons, light switches, lift panels, starter buttons, petrol-tank caps, pens, pump-dials, telephone dials . . . All of the objects are concerned with opening and shutting, measuring, linking and separating, permitting or refusing access, and in general with communication. It seems reasonable to say that they are chosen to reflect the impermanence and constant modification of relationships. They echo the credit sequence of a man's and a woman's hands repeatedly clasping, caressing, and unclasping. In certain cases their use is brilliantly related to the psychological situation of the actors. After the moment of recognition in the lift, Pierre switches the light in his room on then off, half-opens the door and then closes it again. This corresponds to his brief glimpse of the possibilities present in the previous scene. When Nicole has telephoned back to accept his invitation, his exhilaration leads him to flood the room with every possible light and walk through every door in the apartment.

After the Lisbon episode, Pierre arrives back at Orly to find his wife waiting for him, and it's not by accident that they are prevented from communicating by a glass panel. A similar feeling is conveyed by the scene where Nicole and Pierre, having retreated from the hotel where they were going to make love, sit disconsolately in their car, their conversation muted by the car windscreen. Pierre's glasses also act as a barrier between him and the world. When Nicole deserts him in the half-built apartment, he retreats behind his glasses for protection. Finally, and perhaps irrelevantly, the constant gear-changes call to mind Truffaut's preoccupation with sudden changes of mood. There are many of these in the film. Pierre, in moments of anguish, frequently finds himself involved in totally ridiculous situations. Franca, who has just seen the photographs of Pierre and Nicole, explodes in fury and berates Jean-Louis Richard who is trying to pick her up. Such a painfully hilarious episode at the heart of the tragedy is a perfect demonstration of Truffaut's theory about the inconsistency and the multiplicity of experience.

But the principal accusation levelled at *La Peau Douce* was simply that Truffaut was regressing to the traditional bourgeois melodrama that he himself had once so severely criticised. Admitting that the subject matter was far from revolutionary, he protested that the anti-romantic and minutely realistic treatment formed the interest of the film. 'The subject of *La Peau Douce* is perhaps the most banal in the world: Him, Her, The Other Woman. The rest? Details, but these details constitute *La Peau 'Douce* . . . You could make a dozen films like it, but they would bear no real resemblance to one another, because no love story resembles any other, by definition . . . Each love story, if it is recounted scrupulously, takes on the value of an example.' Insofar as it constitutes an example, this is also a moralist's film; but even the moral is reactionary, and contradicted the current trend. From a technical point of view, too, if the film provides Truffaut with an opportunity to experiment with a few minor techniques new to him, it is nevertheless basically conventional. The almost subliminal emphasis of the momentarily frozen frames, and the delayed-action camera mechanism, whirring over the scene when Franca opens the films, remind us of what she is about to

see. There is, too, an interesting use of 'subjective time', when the sequence going up in the lift takes 75 seconds (and about 25 shots) while the descent lasts about a fifth of that time.

Conscious of this, Truffaut could say 'I'm well aware that I'm not one of the avant-garde, it's not to my taste, and moreover not within my capabilities. People devoted to modern trends are in general extremely cultured people like Rivette and Godard. As for me, I work with what's established, merely trying not to repeat what's already been done.' By analogy, he could now take a reactionary stand even on the question of the *cinéma d'auteurs*; publicly regretting the passing of the scenarist's cinema, he said: 'It's now apparent that too many different and often contradictory qualities are necessary in this job. Look what happened in the American cinema. When certain authors became free, their films deteriorated. It's a shocking thought, but a fact. The Hollywood system of a scenario ready to shoot and of the editing out of the director's hands worked well eight out of ten times . . . Such a system was an injustice in the case of a genius like Welles, but that's only an exception.' This complete reversal, when contemporary opinion was still in the process of adopting his earlier view, combined

La Peau Douce: *love in the form of worship.*

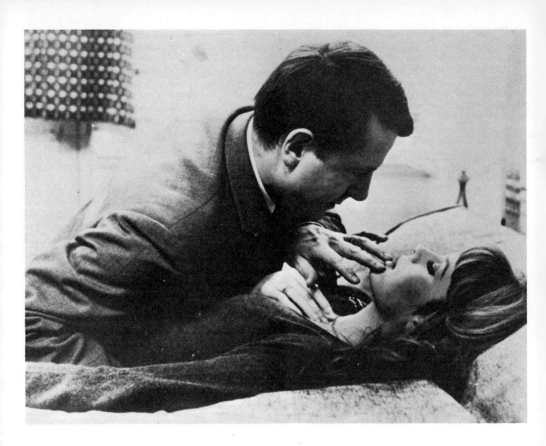

La Peau Douce: *Pierre on thin ice: a glacial passion is the limit of Pierre's romantic interlude; Pierre inherits Charlie's timidity, Nicole Catherine's opacity.*

with the comparative failure of *L'Amour à vingt ans*, *La Peau Douce* and *Fahrenheit 451*, gave his many enemies ample ammunition for sarcastic attacks and brought about a temporary eclipse in his career. In fact the poor reception of *La Peau Douce* was totally unjustified: only the last ten minutes are open to question, perhaps because the violence is incongruous and superfluous, perhaps because the tragedy depends on an arbitrarily delayed phone-call that smacks of script-writer's vindictiveness; but also because of one inexplicable lapse of taste – the forced melodrama of Pierre's restaurant sequence intercut with his wife's whirlwind drive through the city towards him, accompanied by florid music. Aside from this momentary lapse, *La Peau Douce* succeeds completely in what it set out to do. It is the Truffaut film most in need of rehabilitation.

Fahrenheit 451

Since Méliès, science fiction has not occupied a position of any importance in the French cinema. It was an unknown field to Truffaut, but in an argument with Raoul Lévy, the producer, who was trying to convince him of its possibilities, he became fascinated by an account of Ray Bradbury's *Fahrenheit 451*. Towards the end of 1960, he read it. As a result, he had Jules and Jim watch a World War I documentary where a pile of books is burnt, and commenting 'Now if they're going to start burning books . . . might as well throw in our hand . . .' In a burst of optimism occasioned by the success of *Jules et Jim* he bought the film rights in June 1962, and early in the next year set about writing the scenario with Jean-Louis Richard. But the big budget involved, and the critical implications of the subject were enough to put off producers. Fortunately for him, in June 1963 the American producer Lewis Allen agreed to buy the rights from him and arrange finance with an undertaking that no one but Truffaut should direct the film. Having shot *La Peau Douce* as a stop-gap, Truffaut expected to go to the United States in 1964 to make the film there, but it took two years to raise finance and Truffaut spent the intervening period preparing his book on Hitchcock. He says he looked at Brasilia, Stockholm, Toronto, Chicago and Meudon for a suitable location; finally he resigned himself to making it in a studio, because of the number of sets that would have to be burnt. In 1965, Universal selected it as the first of a series of films to be made under contract to them in England.

The film was, then, something of a landmark in his career: his first science fiction, his first colour film, his first studio-made film, and the first of his films to be made in a foreign language –

one which he could not speak. It was therefore risky as well as costly, and again he chose to rely on professional actors. Oskar Werner was to star because Truffaut had such pleasant memories of their collaboration on *Jules et Jim*, but he hesitated about the women's roles. He had seen Julie Christie's photo in a newspaper report on young English women. He suggested her to the producer and they had her latest film projected. Both thought her outstanding, so when Truffaut was next in London where she was making *Darling* he went to see her. He proposed the role of Linda; Julie Christie preferred that of Clarisse. For these two roles Truffaut had decided to find two actresses who looked alike, since he considered physical differentiation for psychological contrast a facile and unnatural technique; the idea then arose of using one actress for both roles.

The book is set in an imaginary society far in the future, in which firemen, instead of extinguishing fires, light them. Their job is to hunt out and incinerate all books, for reading is regarded as a subversive activity. It had been written in 1953, while the House Committee on Un-American Activities was still in progress. Truffaut's frequent statements of his devotion to books and films make apparent how sinister the concepts expressed in *Fahrenheit 451* must have seemed to him. Already in *Les Quatre Cents Coups,* Antoine had nearly burnt the house down through lighting candles by the icon he had set up to honour Balzac. He defended the subject of the new film in an interview: 'The theme of the film is the love of books. For some this love is intellectual: you love a book for its contents, for what is written inside it. For

81

Fahrenheit 451: *the fire-engine in the rescue of people's minds.*

others it's an emotional attachment to the book as an object. This might be the case for a person who had in his childhood been deprived of books or perhaps who nostalgically associates a certain book with a birthday present or a school prize. Thus, books become objects of particular affection; time passes, the binding, the cover, the very smell of the pages takes on a special extremely evocative meaning. On a less individual and intimate level, the story interests me because it is a reality: the burning of books, the persecution of ideas, the terror of new concepts, these are elements that return again and again in the history of mankind. Once, they were expressed cruelly, openly. Now they are manifested more obscurely, more discreetly, but more dangerously. . . . Records, tapes, cinema, TV, transistor radios . . . we watch, we listen. Alienating operations which project us outside ourselves, deprive us of

the time for reflection, the solitude which the intellectual operation of reading involves . . . In our society, books are not burnt by Hitler or the Holy Inquisition, they are rendered useless, drowned in a flood of images, sounds, objects. And the intellectuals, the real ones, the honest ones, are like Jews, like the Resistance; if you're a thinker in a world of objects, you're damned; if you have new ideas, you're a heretic; if you're different, you're an enemy. A person who creates a crisis in society because he acknowledges his bad conscience – the living proof that not everyone has lost his reason, not everyone has betrayed in exchange for a country house, for a car, or for a collection of electronic gadgets – he is a man to eliminate along with his books.'

Like Bradbury, Truffaut and Richard kept the Occupation and the French Resistance constantly in mind when writing the scenario; for them, Montag was a member of a gestapo – Fire Service, here – who begins to sympathise with the Resistance without letting it interrupt his routine gestapo activities. They also kept in mind the Inquisition, and religious intolerance in general: there is something deliberately reverent in the way Montag is helped on with his robes for the first burning of books. Truffaut compared him with an archbishop at this point, and the firemen themselves look like black-robed priests.

Truffaut cites two incidents that occurred while they were raising finances as proof that the theme was still relevant to present conditions. On 2 May 1964 the Indonesian authorities organised an

Fahrenheit 451: *the Captain (Cyril Cusack) and Montag (Oskar Werner).*

immense bonfire of books disapproved of by the Government. The other incident which affected him more personally was the banning of *La Réligieuse*, Rivette's second film, by the French Government. The Censorship Board itself had twice refused to ban it, despite a request for reconsideration of their decision by the Minister. At least Godard's second film, *Le Petit Soldat*, had been banned legally, through official channels. But now, the Government was acting on the eve of an election, subject to pressure from religious authorities, who had never seen the film in question themselves. Godard published a scathing open letter to Malraux in Le Nouvel Observateur, and Chabrol attacked the decision in Paris Presse. Truffaut made constant reference to the incident as an indication of the natural repressive tendency inherent in the idea of society. This was why he included along with a copy of Cahiers a picture of Anna Karina in her nun's habit, on one of his bonfires, regretting only that no copy of the book itself had been available.

Although none of Truffaut's films is overtly political, for he is temperamentally incapable of supporting any one faction to the exclusion of all others, there is a degree of political inspiration behind this film – sufficient for him to say: 'It is, if you like, what might be called politics-fiction rather than science fiction, because there is no doubt that book-burners are all around us. In France, when the authorities ban *La Réligieuse* they are acting out the role of book-burners. It's a political problem, it's politics. I'm against society, but not in a fanatical way; I'm against the notion of society. If I were a Polish director, I'd be against Polish society, if I was Czech . . . or Russian . . . For me, an artist need not necessarily be in open conflict with authority, but he must be *against*, sceptic, someone who protests, who doubts.' *Fahrenheit 451* is the account of the development within an authoritarian society of just such a doubter. Yet we never really get to know Montag as we usually do with Truffaut's characters. His personality is not presented in the loving detail that we are used to, and even his conversion to the ranks of booklovers can seem unconvincing, product of a chance question from Clarisse and a few words arduously deciphered in a novel. In fact, for Truffaut, the very sight of a book, and the fact of handling it, would reasonably result in total devotion to it. 'As in my other films, he's a person caught up in a mechanism. He exists in his own little world, until suddenly something goes haywire. From the moment he takes home a book and begins to leaf through it, he's caught in that mechanism. Only whereas it all seems to me terribly logical and inevitable, it may appear un-

Fahrenheit 451: the civilised child learns to read, gains consciousness.

natural to the spectators. That's what happened with *La Peau Douce.'*

Part of the trouble is that, for the first time, Truffaut's starting point was neither a person nor a relationship, but an abstract concept, an opposition of ideas. Throughout the writing of the scenario and the filming, Truffaut struggled to make the characters less schematic. His problem was basically similar to the one he had faced in *Tirez sur le pianiste* and in *Jules et Jim,* both of which were strong simple situations, borrowed from someone else, which he then proceeded to assimilate, by insinuating elements of his own personality. Here, his first step was to strip the story of its futuristic features. He then introduced elements from the past – an old phonograph on a car, the antique telephone straight out of a Griffith film, dresses copied from the wardrobes used for Debbie Reynolds and Carole Lombard, and the quaint fire-engine out of Frank Capra's *Mr Deeds Goes To Town.* 'Obviously it would be a little abusive to make *Fahrenheit 451* a period film, yet I'm heading a little in that direction. I'm working in reverse; a bit like making a James Bond film set in the Middle Ages.' In general these old-fashioned elements are reserved for those who resist the book-burners' society, such as the old woman or the Bookmen, with their antique caravan. When we see traces of them appearing in the society itself, they suggest infiltration. The flying men are the only survivors of the purge of

Fahrenheit 451: *Truffaut on the set with Cyril Cusack and Bee Duffell; burning books means burning people.*

all futuristic gadgets. The result is an odd blend of the recent past and the near future – our own society, slightly distorted. 'Ultimately I think it's stronger like that, and truer: a normal society, little different from ours except for the simple fact that all reading is forbidden.'

Truffaut did humanise the characters, who originally formed an abstract pattern of stark moral contrasts. In this he was helped by circumstances, for Oskar Werner played the misunderstood husband rather more impatiently than Truffaut had intended, so that Montag appeared less sympathetic. Moreover the Captain, who is thoroughly objectionable in the book, became more humane and understanding. The result was a less clearcut opposition between hero and villain, which Truffaut was glad to see. When Montag finally incinerates the Captain, it is no longer possible to see it in simple terms as a victory of good over evil. This also applies to the old woman who refuses to leave her books, preferring to burn with them. A forceful personality could easily have made this role into a cliché, the old woman representing the Noble Guardian of Civilised Values. To avoid this, Truffaut chose a little fat woman who seems, if anything, more ridiculous than noble. There is only the discreetest of references to her courage, in the copy of Michelet's 'Jeanne d'Arc' burning at her feet with a photo of Jean Seberg in the Preminger film. Always Truffaut rejects the obvious solution: instead of exploiting the strong situations which had originally attracted him, he humanises them with details.

The same principle is at work in the female roles. The idea of using Julie Christie in two parts, one of which is totally subject to the system while the other revolts against it, obviously appealed to him because it introduced an element of moral confusion into the originally simple opposition. It implies that both attitudes are potentially present in each of us, that they are both sides of one coin. Extending this idea, Truf-

faut filmed Linda predominantly in profile, whereas Clarisse is nearly always seen full-face. 'I wanted to equalise the two female characters. Linda was something of a caricature: I humanised her. On the other hand I removed some of the poetic nature of the role of Clarisse by making it more specific, by giving her a job. Now you know where she comes from, where she's going. In the same way Montag is not a hero: I feel incapable of filming a hero.'

If there is a hero in the film, it is the books themselves, which begin to seem as vulnerable as living beings. They are never defended openly; this would have made the film too obviously 'moral'. 'In my film, the only arguments placed in the dialogue are those *against* books, and in my opinion they're sound. When the Captain says, for example, that philosophy is a question of fashion, or that writers write first of all out of necessity and secondly out of vanity. There are no arguments given in favour of books: Montag listens to the Captain without reacting. I've filmed the books in such a way that they provide their *own* defence, that you feel they are living things, and that they can die.' In fact his dissatisfaction with some early scenes was finally traced to the fact that he had allowed books floating through the air to fall out of frame; in the circumstances, this was the equivalent of leaving a person's head out of frame. In previous films, whenever he talked of 'privileged scenes' – which were to be given weight at every stage in the making of the film – it was always in connection with substantiating the human relationships, the moments of contact between people. Here, when he talks of such privileged scenes, he is invariably referring to the burning of books, and wondering how to increase our sense of horror at such an atrocity. There are three such scenes in the film, and each time the camera goes in a little closer, in an attempt to intensify our relationship to them. For these scenes he also borrowed a technique from Hitchcock, 'because they resemble crimes, and Hitchcock is the director who pays most attention to crimes': cutting back and forth between different versions shot by several cameras, to give an impression of agitation.

Fahrenheit 451: *Clarisse (Julie Christie) thinks dangerous thoughts.*

Fahrenheit 451 bears very little resemblance to the preceding films, based primarily on the general topic of love. Truffaut even removed all sexual associations from the character of Clarisse, because he felt he had sufficiently treated the subject of adultery in his two preceding films. In dealing with individuals in a state of cultural deprivation, it looks forward to *L'Enfant Sauvage*, and is more closely connected to *Les Quatre Cents Coups* than to the intervening films. *Les Quatre Cents Coups* showed an individual rejected by society, clinging to cultural values. *Fahrenheit 451* does the same, but here culture and society are more clearly portrayed as mutually incompatible.

Like Catherine and Colette, the principal woman is associated from the beginning with the enduring world of art: literature, this time. In following her, Montag is led out of the constricting city environment towards the liberating influences of nature, where he will become reconciled to life as Antoine had hoped to be at the end of *Les Quatre Cents Coups*. The difference between this and the earlier film is that, unlike *Tirez sur le pianiste*, *Jules et Jim* and especially *La Peau Douce*, it represents the triumph of nature: the visionary land actually exists, and the ideal woman who leads Montag to it will never disillusion him. In this, *Fahrenheit 451* is clearly a more optimistic film than the increasingly pessimistic ones that had led up to it; but then it is basically a fable, and 'a fable proves nothing, cannot prove anything'. The affirmations of the ending are not a real possibility in the literal sense, for this dream had been dealt with in *La Peau Douce*; they are rather a salutary ideal to keep in mind, to help one through the sordid compromises of life. Therefore, it is perhaps not justified to talk of optimism, except to the extent that Truffaut himself modified the end. In the book, Clarisse disappears relatively early on, and Montag escapes, to see the city across the river wiped out in an enormous explosion.

Filming was due to start on 10 January 1966, but was delayed a week to allow Julie Christie to recover from *Doctor Zhivago*. It took thirteen weeks, of which one was spent in France near the experimental monorail at Châteauneuf-sur-Loire. Few special effects were necessary, but the flying men were, of course, suspended from wires, which were subsequently erased from the image. The scene where the Captain is consumed by flames was shot with a glass screen between the flamethrowers and their target. On the other hand, the old woman did have to 'die' within a few feet of her burning books, which required some courage. In both cases, dummies were filmed as the characters were consumed by the flames. In general, the fire scenes could be shot only once, since the sets were burnt with them, but they were filmed by up to six cameras to provide enough material.

It was these fire scenes that had originally suggested the use of colour, but Truffaut was forced through a commercial commitment by Universal to use the Technicolor process, which he didn't particularly admire. Ideally, he would have chosen the Trucolor used in Nicholas Ray's *Johnny Guitar*. As it was, he asked his photographic team for an image as far removed as possible from bland pastels, with prominent areas of hard bright colours. Montag's flat contains large areas of yellow and blue and the firemen's world predominantly consists of blocks of red and black, the colours of fascism. The overall effect is reminiscent of a child's toybox, and this was intentional. With a month of shooting behind him, Truffaut notes in his journal that emphasising the playful aspect, to make it all seem an elaborate game, was a better way of involving the audience than belabouring

Fahrenheit 451: Montag destroys his captain, dangerous action.

Fahrenheit 451: *Montag with his wife Linda (Julie Christie); three stages of consciousness – catatonia, anxiety, then salvation, for Montag, near-suicide for Linda.*

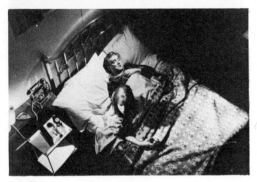

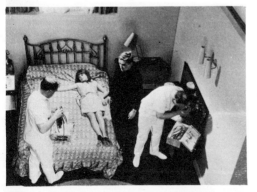

them with solemn moral pronouncements: 'Two months ago, in scenario form, this was a harsh, violent film, packed full of fine sentiments and rather solemn. While filming it, I've become aware of a temptation to give it a certain lightheartedness; consequently I've come to see it more objectively, to treat the future as I treated the past in *Jules et Jim,* not forcing the public's hand or insisting that they take it all too seriously. If I began the film again, I'd say to the decorator, the dresser, the cameraman, 'let's make a film on life as it's seen by children, the firemen will be lead soldiers, the fire-station a splendid toy, and so on . . .' Certainly, the flat colours reinforce the idea of the firemen's world as one of simple, crude concepts, without shades of meaning or qualification. On the other hand, when we meet the Bookmen, we are surrounded by softer shades of green and brown. The white of the snow was purely fortuitous, yet it reminds us of the drive into the snowclad mountains at the end of *Tirez sur le pianiste*; there as here, the purity of whiteness was associated with the existence of this ideal world.

These final scenes caused him many problems. Until the last moment he had no idea what tone to adopt in them. 'If I were a believer, I'd pray this evening for fine weather tomorrow and a good idea during the night.' If he treated them too solemnly, they would make it look like a *film à thèse*, pushing pompous humanist propaganda. Truffaut had, throughout, tried to keep this *grand sujet* down to human proportions, and decided to play down the ending by including as many humorous touches as he could. As a result, the final scenes are whimsical in tone, the Bookmen are introduced casually and, lacking any sort of formal climax, the film seems to fade out rather than end. It is possible this was an attempt to tone down the apparent optimism of the ending. It is equally possible it was simply a product of the indecision Truffaut admitted at the time. Certainly, the Bookmen somehow suggest a formal ballet, and constitute no real alternative to the formalistic society Montag has fled. In the end, the fable seems to have triumphed over Truffaut's humanising tendencies.

A further, more serious, problem had been affecting the progress of the film ever since the early stages: a conflict had developed between Truffaut and Oskar Werner, who had, in the five years since *Jules et Jim,* developed fixed ideas about the autocracy of the actor and viewed the director as an upstart in the dramatic world, even trying to get Julie Christie and Cyril Cusack to change their interpretations to fit his. He also refused to act in any scenes involving fire. After several violent arguments he retired to his dressing room and Truffaut was obliged to use his double more and more frequently. Within a month relations had deteriorated to the extent that the mild-mannered Truffaut describes himself as saying: ' "We have to put up with one another till the end of April. This is not turning out to be the film you wanted, nor the film I wanted, but something in between. If the scene as I shoot it doesn't please you, you've only to stay in your dressing room and I'll shoot it without you, using your double . . ." He didn't reply, probably because I didn't let him get a word in, and finally did the scene as I wanted it, except for the last reply which he sabotaged and which I'll cut when I do the editing.' He frequently notes that he let small details get by in this way, promising himself that he would correct them in the editing. In particular, Oskar Werner would not do the role as neutrally as Truffaut wanted but tended to exaggerate gestures and expressions for dramatic effect. He was trying to turn Montag into a conventional hero, which was precisely what Truffaut wanted to avoid. 'Five years ago he wasn't at all like that, he didn't try to give his role prestige at any cost, but did his job in an honest and dignified way. Now he would be incapable of playing Jules like that, because he'd want to shine at the expense of Jim and Catherine; in fact he'd refuse the role as unworthy of him.'

Continuity problems were created when Oskar Werner appeared one day with his head practically shaved. The grotesque effect Werner's head sometimes had alongside Julie Christie's smaller one caused difficulty during editing. In the final version they are very seldom seen together in the same frame, which naturally means a lot of intercutting. Working in such conditions was a constant strain, and Truffaut renounced several ideas for scenes towards the end. One minor triumph was achieved during editing, simply by reversing film, so that where Oskar Werner had retreated from the flames with the other actors, Montag seems to walk slowly towards them after the others have left, which is what Truffaut had asked of him. The Captain's voice was added to the sound track, saying 'Montag, come back!'

Problems arose, too, as the budget, already large, was increased by delays. For the first time Truffaut found himself subject to strict timetables to ensure maximum use of the studios and the elaborate sets which, nevertheless, often had to be skimped at the last moment because the week's budget had been used up. Regulations required that a crowd of technicians make the trip to France, when only a few actors were needed for four minor scenes. To combat the delays, he instituted a system of editing whilst shooting, which he hoped would allow the two processes to interact, as well as allowing the soundtrack to be added soon after the end of shooting. To reduce the amount of material he was handling during editing, he tried to work with only one take from each scene. The system worked, and the edited version was ready on 18 May, three weeks after shooting was finished. *'Fahrenheit 451* wasn't so much filmed as wrenched into existence, scene by scene.'

Bernard Herrmann, whose music for Hitchcock he had admired, was chosen as composer. Having rejected the futurist aspect of the story, Truffaut didn't want electronic or *musique concréte* but asked for an unostentatious 'neutral' score that would 'escort' the scenes without suggesting anything in addition. When they added up the minutes of film needing music, they found that exactly half of the final version was free of dialogue. 'I shot the film in English, but that's not why it's largely silent: it simply seemed to me a strongly visual story. I'd just done the chats with Hitchcock, and had much admired in his latest films, particularly in *The Birds,* the percentage of purely visual scenes and the progressive elimination of all explanatory scenes.'

For once it is not really relevant to enumerate the quotations from diverse sources, mainly literary, that appear in the course of the film: most of them are readily apparent, and have no justification except an evocative title, author, or format; several books are present only because they happen to burn rather photogenically. If there are, as he said, more quotes in this one film than in all Godard's eleven put together, only those already mentioned were specifically chosen, along with the opening of *The Master of Ballantrae*; we hear a young boy learning a passage from this about a child deprived of paternal affection. Apart from these titles and texts, there is not a single word printed anywhere in the film, even in the credits. Echoing this struggle between the word and the image, Montag begins to read his first book by the flickering light of a blank television screen, and one of the hiding places chosen for the books is a gutted television set. It is logical that the first thing Montag should burn along with the conjugal bed, is the television.

One final theme that Truffaut introduced into the story is that of narcissism: men hold their own wrists, women kiss their own reflections in windows or caress the fur they are wearing; Linda strokes her own breast. All such gestures are performed by members of the book-burning society: no longer curious, developing, outward-going, but introverted and convinced of the perfection of the present state of things.

First shown to the public at the Venice festival in September 1966, the film won no awards. It opened in Paris a week later to mixed reviews. Even Truffaut's colleagues on Cahiers varied between a non-committal appreciation of intentions and vaguely-worded enthusiasm. Bradbury himself, who had nearly been tempted to overcome his fear of plane-travel to watch the shooting, was sufficiently enthusiastic to say 'François Truffaut has given a new form to my book while remaining true to the spirit of it . . . Such fidelity is really miraculous in the cinema', and to send him a scenario of his Martian Chronicles which he himself had sketched out. As for Truffaut, he was at

Fahrenheit 451: Montag and Clarisse and the monorail at Châteauneuf-sur-Loire.

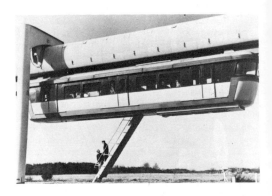

least satisfied with the overall construction of the film, finding the succession of scenes harmonious: 'It would be almost impossible to displace them. One scene I suppressed created such an obvious gap that I had to fabricate a new one during the editing out of unused scraps from other sequences in the film.' But the individual elements considered separately did not please him so much: 'I have a very poor opinion of this film taken scene by scene, shot by shot, but to enumerate all the ugly features I've allowed to creep in would smack of masochism, especially now I'm spending six hours a day trying to edit them out.' In general, the critics found it dry, lacking in the warmth they had come to expect from him. As he had foreseen, they considered the conflict between subject and style disconcerting: this conflict had been at the basis of his decision to make the film. He had taken a science fiction story and treated it more like contemporary reality; he had introduced into a

Fahrenheit 451: *Montag, Clarisse and a Bookman: the happy ending.*

moral fable something of the complexity of real people; on top of this, he had begun with the most serious of intentions but found himself veering more and more towards light-heartedness during filming. Although the underlying intention of the film had to be preserved intact, the treatment of individual episodes was constantly being modified to attain a blend of many elements which reflects, as far as a given story allows, the multiplicity of experience. 'My films are born of an intention to concoct a mixture, of a desire to attempt a new blend of pre-existing elements . . . In the case of *Fahrenheit 451*, it was a question of treating a fantastic story in an offhand way, making the fantastic seem banal and the banal seem odd . . . At each stage of making a film I have to fight against the preceding stage. This scenario was written to give the maximum of plausibility and rationality. But while shooting, each time I came to a realistic scene I tried to give it a trace of craziness; and on the other hand, a frightful scene like the book-burning had to be treated as a documentary. The scenario was written to inspire fear, to be affecting, but during shooting I couldn't take it altogether seriously. I put in any little thing that amused me . . . I don't know yet if the result will look like a normal film shot by a madman, or a mad film shot by a normal man, but I'm convinced that the very fact of writing books and making films makes us abnormal people who are trying to communicate with normal people. Sometimes our madness is accepted, sometimes refused. Since I realised that, the question of whether my films are successful or not occupies me less and less; and I'll never again feel as I did with *Les Quatre Cents Coups,* so afraid of not interesting anyone . . . My slowness forces me to shoot only a third of my projects, but I think I still have a lot of mixtures to concoct, new blends to try out. I have thirty films to make in the course of my life: some will succeed, others not, and that's of little concern to me, as long as I'm allowed to make them.' The theme of *Fahrenheit 451* is precisely this right of the individual to communicate his ideas to the society he lives in, however distasteful that society may find them.

La Mariée était en noir

It was five years since his last major success, *Jules et Jim*: the pressure to choose a popular subject was increasing. Aside from this, three factors guided his choice. The first was Jeanne Moreau: 'It's only on the editing table that you really begin to discover an actor, to really get to understand them and appreciate their possibilities; that's why it's always necessary to make two with those you like.' For this second film centred on her: he did not simply want to repeat his achievements in the earlier one, preferring to wait until he found for her a role which had nothing whatsoever in common with Catherine. This was difficult because, reacting against the 'intellectual sulkiness' that had been required in such films as *Moderato Cantabile* and *La Notte,* he had then asked her for a wide range of expression. To avoid repetition, they would need to find an impassive, neutral part and in 1964 he spoke to her of a novel by William Irish in which there was this kind of character. He couldn't remember the title, but knew it was a murder story he had 'borrowed' from his mother, just after the Liberation. He described the murder scenes he remembered, and enlisted her help in finding it. By chance, it was republished soon after by the Presses de la Cité, and it was as good as he remembered it.

It had a further advantage in six male roles that were suitable for several actors whom he had been wanting to use for a long time. The exact nature of the roles could be varied at will to fit the actors engaged. But the third and main reason was the novel itself, because Truffaut felt that the authors of gangster stories have a creative freedom unknown to 'serious novelists' since they are not subject to criticism and analysis in

La Mariée était en noir: *the widow wore white: Julie and her husband David (Serge Rousseau).*

literary periodicals. Besides, they usually deal with isolation and the problems of guilt, which are both central to his own preoccupations. 'Some think that in adapting Goodis and Irish I'm admitting an obsession with a minor literary form, whereas in my opinion they write much better novels than those proposed to me: "L'Etranger," "La Truite," "La Motocyclette," "La Chamade" and other fashionable books.' For him authors of gangster stories are poets. If on the whole Goodis's themes were closer to his own, he could, nevertheless, see how to appropriate the Irish novel, making the result a homage to the American cinema with which he felt he had not yet entirely squared his debt.

The most important thing that such a novel could provide was a strong, tight plot. 'What strikes me when people talk about my films is that they use words like "discretion" and "half-tones", as if to say that there's no action in them. So I'm tempted to take stronger and stronger events just to see if they still think nothing happens.' Admitting that nothing happened in *L'Amour à vingt ans,* he had shown a murder in *La Peau Douce*: the film had been judged austere. In *Fahrenheit 451* he showed two people being burned alive: it was judged dry and undramatic. Because he had just published his 'endless interview' with Hitchcock, it was inevitable that the choice should be attributed to this influence, and to a certain extent the inference is justified. The film shares Hitchcock's preoccupation with presenting crimes visually; the audience's reaction is deliberately manipulated. Truffaut himself has characterised the four major murders as follows: 1) what does she want with him? Good heavens, she's killed him; 2) hell, she's going to kill him, too; 3) well, well, it didn't go the way we thought it would, that time; 4) she'll get caught this time . . . oh no, I thought . . . 'All the time you must keep count of the public's reasoning. You say to yourself, I'll make them think that . . . that she's

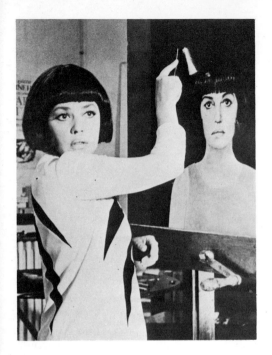

La Mariée était en noir: *Julie removes Fergus's paintings.*

fallen in love with Charles Denner, for instance.' We feel that she's going to use the knife to stab someone, when she's only going to cut the wires; she uses the razor simply to slice out the paintings. Like Hitchcock, he is playing on the audience's primitive fears. Equally reminiscent of Hitchcock are the numerous neatly linked shots, like the rapid progression from scarf to plane, to her inside it, to her view of the city, then her in a room in that city. But such devices for tightening up the scenario had been present in Truffaut's much earlier films. In *Tirez sur le pianiste*, Truffaut had solved the problem of constructing the milk-bomb scene by asking himself

'How would Hitchcock tighten up this scene?' The result is that the windscreen wipers clear away the milk, to show Charlie escaping along the footpath. Truffaut himself has argued that Hitchcock's influence is in a sense *less* in *La Mariée était en noir* than in the preceding films, since the book already developed in the manner of a Hitchcock film: all Truffaut had to do was to see that this was preserved in the scenario. In *La Peau Douce*, on the contrary, where the scenario was constantly in danger of falling apart, and in *Fahrenheit 451*, where the characters were such abstractions that the audience might well not feel involved in their actions, deliberate recourse to such techniques was frequently necessary.

If anything, Truffaut worked in the opposite direction here, by attempting to humanise the thriller and thus *attenuating* the dramatic element. His normal procedure is to write the scenario 'against' the book. Here, he was aiming at an American story treated in a French way, a Hitchcock story treated in the manner of Renoir, a strong situation treated as a character study. Inevitably the result would to some extent resemble *Tirez sur le pianiste*, where he had taken a strong situation from similar sources and humanised it as a study of timidity. 'There are two sorts of film: films of situation and films of character. It struck me that it should be possible to mix the two, so I tried to make this rather extravagant story realistic. It's a sort of Walt Disney for grown-ups. I like making films that resemble fairy tales.' Truffaut's problem was that each victim had a maximum of a quarter of an hour to exist for us. These episodes would inevitably resemble 'sketches', linked by the Bride. The Bride herself is not a real person, but rather a symbol of absolute happiness through love which has tempted his men since the first films. In *Jules et Jim*, we saw her grow into the role. Here, the dream has already been destroyed at the outset: the possibility of realising such an ideal has died with her husband, and she is left to revenge his death, with an intensity which reflects the intensity of her love for him. She expresses this very briefly, at the end of the third episode, for Truffaut felt his characters had sufficiently expressed it in earlier films and he was pleased to be filming a love story where there is not a single kiss or embrace; yet it is apparent that this lifelong passion that has been destroyed before the story begins played a large part in deciding him to make the film.

In the course of her vengeance, the Bride is likened to Diana the huntress; she also represents Death, the incarnation of an implacable destiny, in much the same way as Maria Casarès had incarnated this in Cocteau's *Orphée*, another 'fairy tale for grown-ups' much admired by Truffaut. For the men, the irruption of the absolute into their lives is at once fascinating and terrifying. Truffaut has said that the five men provided him with an opportunity to portray five ways of looking at women; to seduce the men, the woman adapts herself to their various conceptions of womankind. The first, Bliss, like Corey, has been a ladykiller; the third, Morane, is a rising politician, and would like an adoring, capable wife, to appreciate his all-embracing wisdom; the fifth, Holmes, is a petty crook, and she adopts the disguise of a brazen slut to seduce him. But in each case she signifies the realisation of a lifelong dream, an ideal which the men had never really imagined could exist in concrete form.

La Mariée était en noir: *(above) Fergus (Charles Denner) adjusts Diana's bow; (left) Julie in the kitchens ready for her last victim.*

This is seen most clearly in the second and fourth episodes, which carry the most conviction. Coral, in the second episode, is as timid as was Charlie the pianist, and life has taught him not to expect much. The only successes he has had with women have been imaginary, and the Bride appears out of nowhere, and acts in accordance with laws he only half-comprehends. Fergus, the artist, is the other victor in whom we recognise elements of Truffaut himself. When he suggests taking her to the cinema, we realise he holds a privileged position in Truffaut's affections. Fergus seems for a moment capable of turning aside Julie's vengeance.

In thus building up the characterisation and emphasising the relationships, Truffaut had to make some sacrifices. In the book, Julie's reason for murdering the men is only revealed at the end. Truffaut suggests it in the second episode and reveals it in the third. The result is to satisfy the

La Mariée était en noir: *Corey (Jean-Claude Brialy)*.

able, frightened men. Only his male characters reveal this fundamental lack of confidence: the women are all manipulators, strong and confident with an instinctive certainty inspired by the absolutes they consciously or unconsciously represent. Alongside them his men often seem incompetent, merely playing at being politicians, at being lecturers, at being artists, at being important. And whenever his films are centred on such a figure, as in the case of *Tirez sur le pianiste*, *La Peau Douce*, *Fahrenheit 451*, and then *La Sirène du Mississippi*, they fail commercially. 'Every time my films have centred on a child, a young man or a woman, they've been accepted by the public, whereas my failures always had adult men as heroes. Each time I show a man of 35, he's refused: people say "No, his behaviour's ridiculous, it's *childish*". I think it all stems from people having a false idea of adults: they believe in adult-adults, whereas there are only adult-children.' This perspicacity fails him when it comes to women, whom he often seems incapable of viewing in the same light, as fallible precarious grown-up girls.

principal source of the spectator's curiosity, and Truffaut has to work hard to build up the suspense anew, by introducing another element of doubt: will Corey realise in time who she is and prevent her from killing the last two? This is a change for the weaker, and reminds us that Truffaut's interest lies elsewhere than in the narrative or the suspense. In fact, this early revelation of the Bride's motive was rendered necessary by another alteration in the plot introduced by Truffaut: in the book, the five men are innocent, and Corey's guilt is revealed just in time to save the last of the victims. But innocent people who can be frightened out of their wits have never held the slightest interest for Truffaut, who requires a certain measure of guilt before he can begin to sympathise with his characters.

In *La Mariée était en noir*, the guilt is largely accidental, but it serves to introduce ambiguity and moral confusion: his characters are vulner-

The making of the film was delayed because the rights were held up in America. While arranging to free them, Truffaut and Jean-Louis Richard set about constructing a scenario from the book. In the meantime, Godard used the story as the basis of *Made in USA* (1966), just before his plunge into Maoism. The idea of different directors producing a set of variations on a theme, filming their own interpretation of a single story, has long appealed to Truffaut.

In sketching out a scenario, the two men's principal original contribution was to be the character studies of the six male roles. In creating the first episode, between Claude Riche and Jean-Claude Brialy, they kept Harold Pinter's plays in mind; they have the acidulous off-beat dialogue which was required. For the second episode, they turned to the novels of Audiberti (whom Truffaut mentions less frequently only than Balzac and Giraudoux) who excelled, in Truffaut's opinion, in creating lonely bachelors. The third episode was to deal with a detestable politician, portrayed by Michel Lonsdale: they had no difficulty in finding material for this, because the election campaign was in full swing at the time. They simply listened to the radio and built up Morane's monologue from excerpts of actual speeches, particularly those of Jean Dutourd, who unwittingly provided the basis for Lonsdale's monologue in *Baisers Volés*, also. The material for the Fergus episode seems to have been more personal, and of course none was needed for the final victim. These brief but important scenes where the characters were given substance were in several cases left blank in the scenario, and created at the last minute. They were the only major modifications needed, so the shooting of the film proceeded unusually smoothly.

However evocative the dialogues, it was going to be difficult to create the five victims so swiftly. Contrary to the method of *La Peau Douce* (fragmented into some 800 shots), *La Mariée était en noir* has about 400, considerably less than the average film, let alone Truffaut's. 'It's easier for a character to exist in the context of a sequence like this, with a certain number of calculated slack periods, than in a fragmented series of shots. This procedure is rather unnatural to me, but I like forcing myself to do things I'm not used to. The principle of *La Mariée était en noir* is to support these slack periods (when you're getting to know the men as individuals) with a series of extremely strong situations.'

In thus taking an American story and interpreting it in a French way, he was taking a risk. It was a risk that had proved commercially unsuccessful with *Tirez sur le pianiste*. That film's story had been transposed to a French setting, and he felt that this might have been one of the causes of its lack of conviction. This time the exact setting of the action is left unspecified; the timescale also is left vague. In the book, Julie's lethal enterprise begins some two years after the murder of her husband. In the film it is impossible to tell how much time has passed either before she starts or between murders. The effect of this vagueness is to reinforce the fairy-tale aspect of the film. Truffaut wryly re-

La Mariée était en noir: *left to right: Holmes (Daniel Boulanger), Coral (Michel Bouquet), Fergus, Morane (Michel Lonsdale) and Bliss (Claude Rich) engage in man-talk (top) then flee (below).*

ferred to it as his version of Snow White and the Seven Dwarfs.

The blending of American and French elements had another consequence: the American side is visual, the French aural. The story told by the image is different from the story told on the soundtrack. The successive murders are not even remotely reflected in the conversations, which deal exclusively with personalities and relationships.

As Truffaut said: 'If the soundtrack was played over the radio, people would be totally at a loss. They would have no reason for ever imagining that murders were taking place . . . This decision to have the characters talk of matters external to the action is one Hitchcock would never accept: for him, it would be a weakening of the structure. I began with the assumption that the structure was so strong that there's no danger of weakening it, that on the contrary it's better to introduce a touch of reality. I tried to make the characters live, and I think it works from Michel Bouquet on.' In *Fahrenheit 451* he had had to rely on others to introduce the inflections and implications he desired. It was a relief, this time, to know exactly what impression the dialogue would make.

In order to underline Julie's symbolic function, she was to be impassive throughout, in much the same way as Antoine and Charlie had been, and for similar reasons – to reflect the intensity of her past suffering. 'Neither laughing, nor smiling, nor sulking, nor sardonic. She must be neither extrovert nor introvert, but normal, determined. I asked her to act without *coquetterie,* like a man – a man who is concentrating on a job that has to be done.' Jeanne Moreau claimed it was the hardest role she had ever been given, because she never had the impression of acting *with* the men. They were being open and sincere, but her role called for her to conceal her thoughts and motives. She became extremely depressed during filming.

The decision to use colour was not founded on any basic necessity. Now that he was established and could use colour, Truffaut accepted it simply as a more accurate representation of the world. In fact, producers and distributors were becoming prejudiced against black and white films, which were practically unacceptable on the foreign market, and particularly in America. His decision to use black and white two years later, for *L'Enfant Sauvage,* was a provocative and mildly courageous step. Colour is not used very imaginatively in *La Mariée était en noir*; except that the Bride's costumes are exclusively black or white. This idea was suggested by Jacques Rivette as a logical extension of the title, and Truffaut thought it suitably melodramatic.

La Mariée était en noir: *(top) Julie prepares to be Diana in white; (below) in prison black.*

La Mariée était en noir: *Julie contemplates her last victim.*

Begun on 16 May 1967, the film was made in Paris and at Cannes in about nine weeks. It cost about 200 million francs, half of what *Fahrenheit 451* would have cost in France, but a lot of money for a film with only the French-speaking market to rely on. For this reason, Artistes Associés had hesitated to back it, but they needn't have worried: over three months of exclu-sive run ensured its success. Certainly it is not one of his more confessional films, but this was de-liberate: 'I had long believed that when something is very real for you, instinct can be relied upon to communicate it, but I soon realised that even to express something sincere, you have to be circuitous and use half-truths, and the more I see his films, the more I realise that in this field Hitchcock is the best.' But there are analogies with his past films: the sense of guilt rendering his men vulnerable, the contrast between strong women and weak men, that could lead him to say that these murder victims were the *Mistons* grown up; the deadening effect of suffering, the craving for an unworldly ideal, and the inevitable end of this ideal. There is the same imaginary land as in that other fable, *Fahrenheit 451,* and the same formal elements as went into *Tirez sur le pianiste.* The consistency between this and his previous films seemed so obvious to Truffaut himself that he said 'I'm well aware that Jeanne Moreau here and Jean-Pierre Léaud in *Les Quatre Cents Coups* are identical people. One takes a more seductive, less affecting or more abstract form, yet I know they must be the same because it's the same person behind the camera and I feel the same imperious reasons for doing things.'

As in *La Peau Douce,* these 'imperious reasons' are stated less openly than had once been the case, and this tendency was to become more marked in future films. 'What interests me is precisely to *hide* these reasons more and more. I make less and less use of the power that I have as director. The more control I have over what I do, the more I'm tempted to be indirect, feeling perhaps that I can thus give a greater force to what I have to say.' As a result, although both critics and public were to be charmed by his next film, *Baisers Volés,* not many would be so rash as to try to specify exactly what it intended to say.

Baisers Volés

The sole justification given by Truffaut for making his next film was his desire to work again with Jean-Pierre Léaud. Ever since *Les Quatre Cents Coups* he had been tempted to exploit more of his own adolescent experiences, transforming them into what would be a sequel to that film. He had originally renounced the idea for fear of seeming to exploit a success, but used a few of these memories in *L'Amour à vingt ans*. By 1967 he was convinced that he had been wrong to give up the idea and after two formally severe films, onto which he had been obliged to impose his personal preoccupations, he felt the need to turn once again to a film based primarily on characterisation, in which the narrative woud be of little significance. 'The people in it count for most – more than the décor, more than the technique, though obviously it had to be reasonably proficient in execution. It has no connection with what I'd been doing before – in *Fahrenheit 451* for instance, the décor is of major significance. I needed a change. In *Fahrenheit 451* and *La Mariée était en noir*, I had reached the point of treating things that were too abstract, and I needed to come back down to earth. In *Baisers Volés*, the action advances very gently, event after event, all very simple and close to life . . . I had more or less set a time limit on the starting date, so one day I got hold of my friends Claude de Givray and Bernard Revon and we sat down and said "Right: what'll we do with Jeane-Pierre?" For his love-life I said, "We'll put him opposite a girl younger than himself". Then as an afterthought, "And we'll give him what is, I think, the dream of all men, young or old – an affair with a married woman".'

To a certain extent it continues his and Léaud's autobiographies, based in this case on Truffaut's own experience of being drummed out of the army and on his problems of reintegration into civilian life. Military service itself is barely touched on, because the very thought of evoking it in detail revolted him, but also because Claude de Givray had sufficiently expressed their common disgust for all things military in *Tire au flanc,* to which Truffaut had contributed advice and a brief appearance.

The Antoine Doinel we meet here is much the same as he was a few years before, though rather closer to Truffaut himself, for in the meantime Léaud had acquired the ability to adapt himself more completely to the personality of the director. He is, therefore, more gauche and tentative in his relationships with others, and particularly so with attractive women; but still agitated, distraught, unstable, vulnerable and given to the famous *fou-rire*. He is as asocial as ever, unassimilable to any conventional niche in society, and capable, through his bewildered incompetence, of causing radical disturbances in the orderly course of events. Those of his acquaintances we meet are mostly outcasts, on the fringes of society – the long-haired forager in rubbish-bins, the prostitutes, or the ageing private detective. When he comes across the Colette of *L'Amour à vingt ans* and finds her conventionally settled with husband and baby, there is a moment of awkward silence. And whenever this social failure is faced by any self-satisfied representatives of the social order, he stands out as the more memorable. Whether it's the army instructor with his bluff obscenities, or Monsieur Tabard (patterned once again on the pronouncements of the politician Jean Dutourd), totally incapable of acknowledging his own inadequacies, all by comparison with Antoine are made to seem

Baisers Volés: *Antoine (Jean-Pierre Léaud) gets a dishonourable discharge.*

very limited. We first meet the Adjutant in a classroom atmosphere, just as we met the firemen in *Fahrenheit 451*; both are associated by Truffaut with the concept of school (for him that means restriction, indoctrination and oppression). In the scenario Antoine is at this moment credited with the resolution 'never again to undertake any single action which might be useful to his country'.

Despite this, Antoine (like Truffaut) is not an angry young man in open revolt, but basically peaceful and tolerant. He is full of such conflicting tendencies: obtuse, yet at times singularly cunning; gauche, yet occasionally suave, often hesitant, yet just as often unjustifiably self-confident. He can see the humorous side of most situations, but has total inability to see the humorous side of his job as detective. Ashamed neither of the job nor of his singular incompetence he perseveres valiantly but unavailingly. Though at home with

a television set, he is not modern in any sense of the word: he would have been more at ease in the last century, judging from his enduring taste for Balzac. 'Antoine Doinel is a living anachronism, a youth from the 19th century totally out of his element amidst the children of Karl Marx and Coca Cola.' In this too he is clearly closer to Truffaut than to Léaud, who could be aggressively contemporary for Godard, as in *Masculin Feminin*: 'I don't deal with the modern period. If you like, there is the same difference between *Masculin Feminin* and this film as between a jerk and a waltz. Me, I'm nostalgic, totally turned towards the past.' Of Godard, Truffaut says: 'I'm sure he never sticks his stamps on the right corner of the envelope – I do.' To some extent, the film's rather dated air is due to the fact that the corresponding events in Truffaut's life took place about 1950-5. Returning to the districts connected with the original events, he was disconcerted to discover them changed, no longer lending themselves to the scenes he had in mind. He feels that in the resulting film there is an underlying conflict between the action and the settings, as if

*Masculin Féminin (above): militant Léaud with
modish girl-friends.*
*Baisers Volés (below): romantic Léaud among the
prostitutes.*

the film were secretly set in 1945, though no one
admits it.

It was partly nostalgia which led him to choose
as theme song one of Charles Trenet's compositions popular during the war years; its gentle
melancholy summarised for him all the confused
memories of his childhood. The song and the film's
title remind us of Antoine's craving for affection:
brought up in deprived circumstances, his reaction
is to seize on all manifestations of affection,
wherever he sees or imagines them. Christine's
family, like that of Colette in *L'Amour à vingt
ans* is an image of something Antoine has never
experienced, and her understanding with her
parents is not the least of her attractions for him.
He makes identically clumsy lunges at the
prostitute and at Christine herself. We are

reminded that already at seventeen he had conceived
an image of love which would render any relationship with a mortal woman unsatisfactory. Although
he knew Christine long before joining the army,
he couldn't reconcile himself to a permanent

relationship with her, because she is too matter-of-fact. We meet in the person of Fabienne Tabard a woman capable of satisfying these romantic longings.

We are once again at the heart of Truffaut's favourite topic – love and particularly the conflict between the absolute and the everyday. As soon as Fabienne appears, she is enshrined amidst the goddesses, alongside Mme de Mortsauf from Balzac's 'Le Lys dans la vallée' which he is seen

Baisers Volés: *Fabienne Tabard (Delphine Seyrig) is flesh and blood.*

reading and which he quotes in his melodramatic farewell letter to her. Truffaut had Delphine Seyrig in mind for this role from the start because her name and presence convey to the public something of the remoteness and the perfection she will represent for Antoine. Recognising the symptoms, pleased with his image of her, yet determined to dispel his illusions, Fabienne pays Antoine an unexpected visit in the course of which she convincingly reassures him that she is neither

symbol nor apparition, but a woman of flesh and blood. She points out to him her efforts of that morning to please her man, and to live up to his image of her, reminding us of the scene in *Jules et Jim* in which Catherine relentlessly removes her make-up, signifying the end of the idyll and the illusions. Antoine's mystification has arisen from his confused definition of 'exceptional', which can seem to indicate 'rare and wondrous', whereas each individual is exceptional. Antoine's idealism, or idolatry, is a distorted form of humanism.

Judging from Truffaut's own obsession with the subject, this step in Antoine's sentimental education will be only temporarily effective, but for the time being, he can devote himself to Christine, accepting relative and specific virtues rather than seeking the imaginary. But the moral receives an ironic twist when, at the very end, a stranger who has been insistently following Christine approaches the reconciled couple on the park bench, and we discover that he has vested Christine with precisely those exotic attributes which Antoine had rejected her for lacking. This scene allows us to foresee future complications for the couple (realised in *Domicile Conjugal*). Christine turns to Antoine and says 'He's a bit crazy', but Antoine is ill at ease: the stranger's protestations cut close to the bone.

* * *

Baisers Volés illustrates the complex stages through which Truffaut's more autobiographical films pass during the preparatory stages, since in this case all the stages except the first are on record. One could roughly enumerate six of them. In the first, ideas for scenes derived from his own experience, or from that of his friends, or from his reading, accumulate in a folder. To these jottings belong, in the present film, the incidents and attitudes in the military prison, the scene with Delphine Seyrig where Antoine says 'Oui, monsieur', and the more general idea for linking together these incidents by making Antoine a private detective. This provides a convenient substitute for the job of journalist which Truffaut had exercised for so long. The incident in which the detective dies in the middle of a telephone call

Baisers Volés: *Antoine plays detective with M. Henri (Harry Max).*

was inspired by an account of the death of the Russian director Dmitri Kirsanoff, who died in this way, his secretary picking up the mouth-piece and saying, 'You might as well hang up: M. Kirsanoff is dead.'

In the second stage, these diverse episodes are written out in a provisional order – not a scenario, but rather a list of ideas. Many are rejected, such as the friend Didier, who had been using Antoine's apartment while he was in the army, and who throughout the preliminary stages was to play a large part in the film. Some of these rejections leave odd traces in the film: the enigmatic young man whom we meet foraging in rubbish-bins may well be the one remaining trace of Didier. Many rejected incidents turn up as mere anecdotes in the film, such as the nurse anecdote or the conversation between Antoine and Paul by the Metro subway. Many incidents survive into the

film because of the fact that they provide variations on the theme of *Baisers Volés*, like the scene of Paul and Catherine in the washroom, Antoine's promenade with a tall girl, or Paul's anecdote. They add to the air of casual disorder that prevails in the sequence of the scenes.

This second stage already contained suggestions for actors and made allowance for their personalities, but it contained no dialogue and ended abruptly, three-quarters of the way through the film, with Antoine bereft of both women: 'From now on Antoine is on his own, since he has had a row with Christine, his adventure with the married woman has come to nothing and he's lost his job; and like him I must admit that I'm rather at a loss, for there are several points to clarify: a) how to round off the adventure with the married woman? b) how to pick up the threads with Christine? (that's easier) c) how to finish off the story from a professional point of view? (instead of resigning, I'd prefer him to be sacked from the agency, but not so as to show him in a bad light).'

of the scenario with the narrative broken up into individual takes, but no indications of techniques to be used and very little dialogue. Even at this stage, more ideas are creeping into the script, such as the rope-trick performed by Jacques Delord, a further homage from Truffaut to the world of cabaret.

It was in the fourth stage, amounting to nine printed pages, that Truffaut showed the scenario to Artistes Associés. They were sceptical, and wanted the estimated cost of this already small-scale film to be reduced even further. One solution would have been to reject the idea of making it in colour, for Truffaut, after using colour for expressive purposes in *Fahrenheit 451*, and using it for purely incidental dramatic purposes in *La Mariée était en noir*, had no precise intentions for it in the present film: 'I didn't add a single coat of paint to anything throughout the film – I even

Baisers Volés *(below): Antoine as the timid detective.*

Baisers Volés *(above): Antoine reads 'La Sirène du Mississippi'.*

The third stage consisted of notes and many hours of tape-recordings, collected by Claude de Givray and Bernard Revon in the course of interviews with shoestore-proprietors, journalists, and detective agencies. From these were salvaged certain techniques for authenticating the jobs Antoine is called on to exercise, and a scattering of anecdotes such as the homosexual who flies into a frenzy of despair on learning that his friend has got married and had a child, the nurse who does a strip-tease, the technique for discovering a person's address, and the idea of a client applying to the agency to find out why nobody loves him. Assimilating stages two and three, Truffaut wrote a coherent outline of the film, in effect a scenario, for it contains detailed character sketches and answers the above three questions (p. 104) in a manner reasonably close to the final version. Between this and the film itself comes a fifth stage, the working version

forgot I was making it in colour.' He decided to make the film in Paris, although his original intention had been to make it in Nice, hoping to escape some of the bitterness of his previous autobiographical films by incorporating into this one something of the sunniness and carefree feel of the south; for despite his personal devotion to Paris, it had always signified resignation and defeat in his previous films, whereas the sun and the sea had suggested tranquillity and hopefulness.

Shooting began on 5 February, but on the 9th Truffaut arrived some hours late on the set because he had been attending a meeting of the council of the Cinémathèque Française, at which Henri Langlois had been ousted by delegates of the Ministry of Culture and the Gaullist Government. Founded by Langlois and Georges Franju in 1936, the Cinémathèque had always been identified with Langlois. Intrinsically unprofitable, since its purpose was to show as many films as possible to as many people as possible, it had been subsidised since 1954 by the Ministry, which had become more and more insistent in making its desires known. In 1968 the Council consisted of twenty-four – eight elected by the hundreds of subscribers to the Cinémathèque, eight appointed by the government, and the other eight co-opted by these sixteeen. Previously, those co-opted had favoured Langlois, but the government managed to get a majority of its own men on the council, and proposed a new director. When the eight or ten (including Truffaut) who favoured Langlois asked for a delay, they were refused and walked out. From then on he fitted in the business of filming only when circumstances permitted. The Cinémathèque had been the only school he respected, and represented all that was worth fighting for in his world. He pointed out that without Langlois and the Cinémathèque there would have been no Cahiers du Cinéma, no Cahiers group, and no New Wave in France. The world-wide renovation which this wave had effected was directly traceable to the influence of Langlois: 'There is the man himself, who is the ultimate in sincerity: he never puts on airs, and we admire that. And aside from the personal questions, there are the films which are in danger, now, because we're dealing with people who know nothing about them . . .'

Langlois was essentially a creator and an individualist, who refused to hand over his creation for official propaganda purposes and the pomp of state visits. The attack on him was based on his incompetence as an administrator, which 'had resulted in films of immense value, often unique in the world, being stored in condemned buildings where the containers were rusting and the films deteriorating and the danger of fire was high.' This 'official report' omitted to mention that Langlois had never been responsible for administration – his job was purely artistic and technical, and the administration was in the hands of one of the government's own men. The films *were* stacked in unacceptable conditions because the Ministry had refused Langlois' appeals for funds to house them better, and had blocked subsidies which could have been used for this purpose. When their own man, Pierre Barbin, took over, these subsidies suddenly became available. Similar methods had already ousted Gaetan Picon, Pierre Boulez, Emile Biasini and other individualists from key posts (Jean-Louis Barrault was to follow soon after) so as to guarantee state control of French music, television, and the Théâtre Français. It was imagined that the takeover of the cinema would go equally smoothly. Barbin had gained control of two of the three leading French film festivals, and had tried for the third; he also had a say in allotting the '*primes à la qualité*'.

On 10 February, Truffaut and about 40 other directors refused a state-run Cinémathèque the right to screen their films; on the 12th the Cinémathèque's attendance was reduced to a trickle; and on the following day it was 'closed for inventory and reorganisation'; on the 14th, about three thousand enthusiasts protested on the Place du Trocadéro, surrounded by thirty bus-loads of police. The riot police broke up the demonstration, and both Truffaut and Godard were hurt. No news of this reached the public, except for an official communiqué which read 'a disturbance was caused by thirty or forty hotheads, spattered with mercurichrome to make it look as if the forces of order had assaulted them'.

Baisers Volés: *M. Tabard (Michel Lonsdale), his shoes and his fantasies.*

A Committee for the Defence of the Cinémathèque was formed under the honorary presidency of Jean Renoir. 'L'Affaire Langlois' had earned bad publicity for the government throughout the world, and many foreign directors had joined with those French directors and producers who forbade the screening of their films. The Cinémathèque had remained closed for over fifty days when the State conceded defeat. On 22 April an extraordinary general meeting of the members voted a return of the Cinémathèque to its pre-1954 status as a private organisation without government representation and with freedom of action.

Inevitably, amidst all this confusion, the filming of *Baisers Volés* took second place: 'I led a double life, ringing up people between each take, giving interviews to foreign networks to compensate for the silence of the ORTF, writing hasty and vindictive articles in *Combat,* going to all meetings of the Defence Committee for which, as Treasurer, I had to take in 50 or so cheques each evening, often missing the projection of the day's takes. The film didn't suffer from it all, I think, perhaps quite the contrary . . . The actors improvised their dialogue, and everyone felt a certain distance from the film, which became

Baisers Volés: *Antoine in the shoe shop.*

a sort of game played whenever we had spare time. Fortunately the principle on which the scenario was based lent itself to this state of mind, and anyway we soon developed a slogan for the film which ran "If *Baisers Volés* is a good film, it'll be because of Henri Langlois, and if it's bad, it'll be because of Barbin".'

He had never begun shooting with so little preparation. Each morning he would spend three or four hours on the 'Affaire Langlois'. Actors would turn up, engaged months before and subsequently forgotten, sometimes for roles he had since dropped. The dialogue, if prepared at all, was written in cafés a few hours or minutes beforehand. What ought to have produced chaos had the opposite effect: a sense of euphoria prevailed throughout the making of the film. Since his days as critic Truffaut had never known a cause so urgent and which so cut through his ability to see all sides of a question. 'For once I was sure of myself: I rather tend to reject life and take refuge in the cinema, so when the cinema is attacked, I must defend it.' The Langlois affair and the filming of *Baisers Volés* were barely terminated, and the Cinémathèque had barely reopened when it was forced to close again, surrounded by the student and police barricades of the May 1968 uprising. As a result, the conflict between cinema and government could seem to have been a symptom of a more general conflict within French society between authority and the individual.

Asked what role the state played with regard to the cinema Truffaut replied: 'The state plays the role of oppressor. It treats the cinema like it treats people – despising the young and the old, and exploiting the rest.' It was in this frame of mind that he played a leading role in bringing the Cannes festival to a halt. The grand gala opening had taken place on 10 May, but in Paris the cinemas of the Latin Quarter had been closed since the 7th, partly because of their location, but also because the spectacle in the street was more entertaining than that in the cinemas. On the night of the 10th, police cleared the streets by using gas and their night-sticks, and a general strike was called for the 13th. The cineastes at Cannes called for the suspension of the festival. After some hesitation, the authorities agreed. It reopened on the 14th. The agitation continued throughout France, and on the 17th, members of various branches of the film industry formed the Etats Généraux du cinéma with a view to reform, and using the Committee for the Defence of the Cinémathèque as the core of the movement. Truffaut, Godard, Jean-Louis Richard, Lelouch and the others thus found themselves 'authorised' to bring the festival to a halt just as technicians were to bring the industry to a halt. On the 18th, they invaded the stage of the main theatre in which *Peppermint Frappé* was, after many delays, about to be screened, cutting wires and in general rendering the equipment unusable. Truffaut himself grabbed the curtains and swung on them, holding them closed.

With the resignation of the jury and the withdrawal of the bulk of the films, the director was forced next day to close the festival. What most pleased Truffaut in this campaign 'was the idea that people were not going to obey, were never again going to obey. I approved also of those who threw paving stones at the riot police, but it wasn't the violence that interested me so much as the imperturbable calm of the action committees, faced with those trying to provoke them . . . of all the events of May, what most struck me was the value of discussion. I was ferociously opposed to talks, but the work of the action committees in the street was devastatingly effective. My second astonishment was that André Malraux didn't commit suicide . . . out of shame . . .'

The Langlois affair and the May uprising served not only to reunite the members of the Cahiers group but also to reconcile cineastes of all generations and all philosophies, many of whom had been at odds for twenty years. It proved, for some, an exhilarating experience. Its effect on Godard can be measured by the direction his films took thereafter: for him, an entirely new cinema had to be created, and anyone who was content to work within the framework of the old forms was worthy only of scorn. Hence the growing coldness between him and Truffaut, on whose films the

events of this period had relatively little measurable effect. In *Baisers Volés*, completed some weeks before the events of May, the Langlois affair received only oblique references: it is dedicated to Langlois and the Cinémathèque, and the credits unroll against a shot of its closed grill. There are also a few remarks from Christine, whose Conservatoire provides a convenient analogy for the Cinémathèque: 'You know, the Conservatoire's closed. They've replaced the director. The pupils preferred the old one and they've boycotted the classes . . .' Later, she has been to a demonstration similar to that in the Place du Trocadéro, and her friend has had to be taken off to hospital – 'You know, they're a disgusting lot. So her father complained to the police headquarters, but they couldn't be bothered even listening.'

The agitation had the effect of making *Baisers Volés* a more relaxed, genial film, for as Truffaut says, it was a means of relaxation: 'All we could do was try to get as much fun out of it as possible, and because I was fortunate enough not to have made any errors in the casting, we managed to get by like that . . . Ultimately it's perhaps a healthy attitude to take from time to time: I only hope it amuses others as much as it did us.' Never since *Tirez sur le pianiste* had Truffaut been so vague as to the precise effect he wanted to achieve; each scene was shot more for itself than for its contribution to the overall pattern. A tendency always latent in Truffaut's films, towards a certain unpredictability in the sequence of scenes, was strengthened. It's impossible to foresee the course that the narrative will take. We get suggestive glimpses, never developed, into people's lives. There is no dramatic necessity for M. Henri's death in the middle of that telephone call, when no one is paying him particular attention; but then, people do die awkwardly, inopportunely and unpredictably.

Another element of realism is the mixture of comic and tragic in what is perhaps the most satisfactory equilibrium he had yet achieved. The breaking down of barriers between dramatic forms was something he had recommended ever since his critical days. He had been disappointed with *Les Quatre Cents Coups* because it turned out

Baisers Volés: *Fabienne Tabard and Antoine; the goddess and her acolyte – Pierre and Nicole in happier circumstances.*

much more sombre than he had intended; *Jules et Jim* similarly dismayed him, and he was forced to admit that during filming a certain melancholy was inclined to creep into even his most comic incidents. Consequently, he decided to base the scenario for *Baisers Volés* almost exclusively on comic scenes, and particulary on violent contrasts of personality. 'We repeatedly put Jean-Pierre Léaud with someone remote from him: a married woman, a 70-year-old detective, a young girl whose modernity contrasts with his anachronistic romanticism. Nothing but extremely strong contrasts. There are only five or six serious scenes in the whole film.' It was his first film with comic pretensions, but the experiment succeeded: the minor-key elements insinuated themselves into the framework more effectively than if tragic and

comic had been formally juxtaposed. 'Once, I thought that some things were funny in life and some things sad, so I put that in my films . . . Later I tried to cut briskly from something sad to something funny. It seems to me today that it is more interesting for the same thing to be both funny and sad depending on the way you look at it. That's one of the reasons I asked Charles Trenet for the right to take as title for the film two words from his song *Que reste-t-il de nos amours*. I think Trenet attained the most perfect equilibrium of gravity and gaiety.' It was this delicately balanced bitter-sweet mood he had aimed at in *L'Amour à vingt ans*. In *Baisers Volés* it is a consistent factor, giving it the coherence it undoubtedly has. Many examples could be cited.

The mirror scene, in which Antoine is seen repeating the three names, begins by being rather amusing, but becomes obsessional and almost embarrassing. The scenes in which the homosexual discovers the truth about his friend, or where M. Tabard reveals his obsessions, are not directed

Baisers Volés: *Antoine and Christine at the end of the film.*

solely for laughs. The men are not caricatures, but presented in such a way that their problems seem real. When Antoine addresses Fabienne as 'Monsieur', there is the same feeling of a traditional comic gag scene, transformed by being set in a real context where we can feel for the characters as well as laugh at them.

Speaking of this scene, Truffaut goes on to say: 'We know perfectly well that Jean-Pierre Léaud is in love with Delphine Seyrig, but we also know that she knows it and that he doesn't know

she knows. There are therefore three in the act: the two of them and the public. With three, it's stronger, more intense . . . There's no hurry . . . The length of the silences makes us expect, I don't know, something crazy . . . perhaps that he'll throw his arms around her and kiss her. I told them both – and it was the only direction I gave them – stir the sugar six times rather than once, wait a while before lifting the cup . . . Then this long wait is climaxed by the "Oui, monsieur", and I think the wrong way to conclude this scene would be fade out and pass on to the next scene. This "Oui, monsieur" is like a train charging along the tracks and there's no stopping it . . . Antoine's only hope is in flight, and he's accompanied by a really frenetic music. I asked Duhamel for the sort of chase music you get in American films, in the hope of preserving this sort of tension that has been created. That's why the music doesn't stop even when someone's speaking, and the camera's on the move all the time. I think that this is one of Hitchcock's lessons: he has a slogan that runs "You've got to put a lot of effort into creating emotion, and once you've created it, even more effort into preserving it . . .".'

It seems strange to hear the name of Hitchcock mentioned in connection with *Baisers Volés* though it is precisely in these 'shapeless' films that he has always fallen back on Hitchcock's techniques.

A more relevant name is Ernst Lubitsch: 'With Lubitsch, I'm attracted by a particular way of treating the scenario, moulding it so as to make it more interesting, relating incidents "by ricochets", in a roundabout way. Apparent throughout the film is the desire to say everything indirectly.' Lubitsch's influence had already been present in *La Mariée était en noir*. Here, no one states openly what they think or feel – it all has to be deduced by the spectator. Similarly, rather than tightening the links between scenes, Truffaut took

Baisers Volés: *Antoine and Christine seal their engagement.*

a perverse pleasure in making them appear the result of an unexpected coincidence. A simple example is the process by which Antoine becomes a private detective: at all costs he must not be made a straightforward verbal offer. So Henri leaves the hotel without any apparent concern for the now jobless Antoine, and it is by accident that they meet again in the café. Again, there is no suggestion of a job; when they leave, we remain inside and see them saying goodbye out on the street. Apparently as an afterthought, Henri turns back and gesticulates. Cut to Antoine trailing a woman, in what is obviously his first case. The calculated casualness of this essential step in the narrative helps to create the air of genial randomness. These devious links most occupied Truffaut's attention during the elaboration of the scenario, much more, in fact, than the incidents themselves. He was particularly worried as to how to get Antoine *out of* the agency; in the final version we merely see him separate from the rest of the agency personnel at the cemetery. The spectator must formulate for himself, if he feels the need, some suitable explanation.

This favouring of a non-committal visual presentation of events is particularly apparent in the last quarter of the film: there is for instance, the delightful hypocrisy of Christine's telephone call to the TV repair service. (In the scenario she was to disable it before ringing, which would have been much less effective.) There is the young couple's progress to bed: the camera silently follows their traces, in much the same way as it does those of Charlie and Thérésa in *Tirez sur le pianiste*. The comparison indicates how Truffaut had learnt to follow his own dictum – that one should never aim at being poetic, but let the poetry grow out of the film if it will. Similarly, next morning, all we need to know about their intentions (and about the preceding night) is conveyed by Antoine's wordlessly slipping a bottle-opener on her finger, as a ring. His distrust of words is evident in the way Truffaut introduces the phrase 'I'll teach you all I know, and you can teach me all you know'. It could sound pompous or sentimental, and so is allowed to arise out of a discussion as to how best to butter dry biscuits. Finally, we are reminded that Antoine, like Truffaut himself, has always combined a reverence for words with a distinct unwillingness to commit himself to them: rather than speak his affection he prefers to convey it in writing. The scenario specifies: 'So as to say important things to each other without speaking, they exchange bits of paper. We never find out what they write on them. Tough luck for us.'

La Sirène du Mississippi

When in *Baisers Volés* we glimpsed Antoine reading a book called *'La Sirène du Mississippi'*, we were unwittingly being subjected to a little pre-publicity. The Hakim brothers had suggested it to him even before he began filming *La Mariée était en noir* (his other adaptation of a William Irish novel) and the project had come to nothing only because, as producers, they reserved the right to modify the film in any way they liked at any stage in the making, a condition Truffaut would not accept.. They had, however, agreed with him that Catherine Deneuve should play the lead role – 'I defy anyone to read as much as three pages without thinking "Ah, she'd be ideal in that" ' – and for two years the Hakims tried to talk her into making it with other directors, including Roger Vadim, but she refused. Their option expired, and late in 1968 Truffaut found himself with the rights at last. Their high cost had been a factor in his decision to make *Baisers Volés* when he did: 'In making *Baisers Volés*, I seem to be giving of the best of myself, before making *La Sirène* as a sort of commercial concession. But the truth is that I shot *Baisers Volés* to earn enough money to acquire the rights of *La Sirène*.'

He decided to use for the first time Jean-Paul Belmondo; they had known each other since *A bout de souffle*. Truffaut had several times considered him notably for *Fahrenheit 451* and in a projected adaptation of Audiberti's 'Monorail'. Deneuve and Belmondo were the best-known and highest paid stars in France; it was already going to be an expensive production with its colour and teams of technicians to be transported thousands of miles. Truffaut had never had anything in principle against high-cost productions, or against star casts. Catherine Deneuve, however, might seem an unlikely choice for a *femme fatale,* a brazen night-club girl; and Belmondo might seem a strange choice for an inexperienced colonial. But 'In *La Sirène* it's his gravity never verging on ponderousness that most interested me, and which gives such intensity to the feelings he expresses . . . There has always been in France a prejudice against the large-scale film, coupled with a feeling that "little" actors are better than the big ones. For me, that's all unimportant. In one film I'll need Léaud, in another Belmondo. I'd be more worried by it if I'd made the film cynically, as a financial calculation: if for example, Belmondo and Deneuve had refused and I'd made it with Bardot and Delon. That's not the case.'

Louis Mahé is directly descended from Antoine, Charlie and Pierre Lachenay in that he is incurably romantic, an idealist who attempts to realise the dreams he has conceived in his island solitude. As with Truffaut's previous heroes, his dreams become identified with a woman. He defines the procedure by which he got to know her – through the marriage columns of a newspaper – as that of an idealist: seeming to leave your destiny in the hands of Fate, you are revealing a craving for the unknown and unpredictable. Antoine himself could not have conceived a more romantic scheme; it would have pleased him because it allowed the romantic ideal to be expressed impersonally, in writing; Louis is as incapable of expressing affection face to face as any of Truffaut's heroes.

When the bride has arrived, and her 'deceit' over the photograph is explained, she seems to fulfil his wildest hopes. She is soft, feminine, and

La Sirène du Mississippi: *Louis (Jean-Paul Belmondo) and Marion/Julie (Catherine Deneuve).*

even more beautiful than he expected. With her bird in its wicker cage, she resembles a fairy-tale princess, and this first section is set in an unreal world, where dreams come true. Louis owns a plantation on the island of Réunion, and the part played by the tropical setting with its white-walled fairy-tale château in lush countryside corresponds to that played in *La Peau Douce* by the Lisbon episode. The photography is slightly over-exposed, exaggerating the tropical light and giving a washed-out look to the colours. On her first

night in the house, however, Julie has a nightmare: she feels choked and stifled by the blackness, and needs a light before she can sleep. This is suggestive of a 'darker' episode in her past, which soon recurs.

Returning home one night, Louis finds she has disappeared with the greater part of his money. Night scenes predominate in the succeeding, longer section, in which reality holds sway, and in which the confusions and practical difficulties occasioned by Julie's obsession with money disrupt the orderly calm of life on Réunion. The first section was static, with few camera movements, and characterised by stillness; the second consists of a series of comings and goings, meetings and part-

La Sirène du Mississippi: *the interlude bought by beauty and wealth; Marion and Louis as neo-colonialists (top); the morning after (middle); Marion as housewife (bottom).*

ings and frequent shifts in fortune, and the camera is more actively used. The dreamer has been rudely awakened; this corresponds to that section in *La Peau Douce* in which Pierre tries to transport back to Paris (and to reality) the vision conceived in Lisbon. From Antibes, Louis and Julie (or more properly Marion) flee to Aix, then to Lyon, where they inhabit a half-constructed apartment building reminiscent of the half-built block of flats in *La Peau Douce* where Nicole announced her intention to break with Pierre; and the last hopes of saving some fragment of the ideal are lost.

Disillusion and death are the inevitable consequence of Louis' attempt to recreate his vision, but in this case the death is not that of a member of the couple, but of the private detective who is getting dangerously close to tracking down Marion. The colours become more ominous: all trace of over-exposure disappears from the photography, and Marion is found wearing a black, spangled evening dress. Her coat makes her resemble a great black bird, and the soft blues and oranges of the first section have become sombre orange-browns and rich blue-blacks.

Comparing her with his original ideal, Louis describes the wonderful letters he had received from Julie, which had seemed to echo his own hopes; instead, he has found Marion, who, as he wryly points out, has brought into his life the 'provisional', where he sought the absolute. His commitment to her is none the less absolute: he fights against the harsh realities she has brought into his life by identifying her with much the same things Truffaut's previous heroes have associated with their ideals. It is in this sense we must read his description of her in terms of a photograph, and of a painted portrait. Art and the ideal have been associated with each other in Truffaut's work since Antoine first refused his real life to take refuge in Balzac's 'La Recherche

La Sirène du Mississippi: *Marion and Louis: in the steps of Pierre Lachenay (see page 80).*

de l'Absolu', and since Jules and Jim saw Catherine prefigured in a sculpted head. Likewise, Louis shuts his eyes to verify Marion's beauty, though she is standing before him, because her reality is in his mind rather than in her mortal body.

It is night when she returns to find the detective dead, and when he returns to Réunion to sell his share in the plantation. Outside his partner's home he pauses to watch through the window, his partner's family enjoying what he has been

obsessed by – because he has never known it – and what he had thought he was about to achieve: a close and comfortable family relationship, a sense of belonging, of permanence, of stability. But, as he says to Jardine, he is of the race of outsiders. The pattern is repeated when he is forced to leave the money behind in the half-built apartment. Moreover, death again threatens with Marion's plan to poison Louis. This would be the equivalent of the end of *Tirez sur le pianiste*, where as here, in a final bid to escape reality the couple set off into the mountains only to find a definitive separation awaiting them. In fact, these are the same mountains, and the hut they shelter in is the gangsters' retreat of the earlier film. The altitude and the snow have the same significance as before, and the shabby hut where the slow murder takes place is sinister in the bright light. Its interior is even more sordid, streaked and splattered with sombre blue-blacks.

Louis realises what is happening, through seeing a comic strip of Snow White and the Seven Dwarfs, in which the poison apple is being produced (Truffaut had called *La Mariée était en noir* his version of Snow White and the Seven Dwarfs). Instead of revolting, Louis accepts his death. Louis and Marion have each accepted death at the other's hands; recognising this common bond and overcome by such devotion, Marion is converted to Louis' definition of love and commits herself to him. His conviction has prevailed over the forces of compromise and resignation, and the last image is of the couple setting off together into the whiteness which was already present in the first section, but which had apparently been dispelled during Louis' attempt to incorporate the dream into their reality. They are going *loin d'ici*, anywhere out of this world, to Lisbon, Réunion or beyond, but certainly crossing a frontier into a new land.

Truffaut has called this an 'open ending', meaning an ambiguous ending, neither optimistic nor pessimistic. A good comparison is the final shot in *Les Quatre Cents Coups*, where we are left with a purely visual image, and the author has not committed himself to whether the promise it contains will be fulfilled or not. Yet a comparison with earlier films shows the end of *La Sirène* to be relatively optimistic. In *Tirez sur le pianiste*, of which this could almost be said to be a remake, the woman dies and Charlie returns full circle to his bar-room piano, forced to acknowledge the unreality of his desires. In the other closely related film, *La Peau Douce*, it is the husband himself who dies. Similar conclusions are reached in *Les Mistons*, *Jules et Jim*, *L'Amour à vingt ans*, and *Baisers Volés*. *La Mariée était en noir* began where these all left off. Only in *Fahrenheit 451* was a vision allowed to take on concrete form, in the land of the Bookmen. Like it, *La Sirène du Mississippi* is a fairy-tale or a fable.

Louis is descended from Antoine, but is also an anti-Antoine figure, allowed to *realise* the dream. Nevertheless a learning process has to be gone through in both cases, for (as Truffaut says) Louis becomes more self-aware and assumes attitudes which had originally been subconscious.

Like Louis, Marion is incapable of any direct expression of affection, and has to fall back on a recorded message which is rather tritely broken. More significantly, however, she uses phrases such as Truffaut frequently uses of his own childhood, phrases which would equally be used by Antoine Doinel. She talks of a childhood deprived of affection, she talks of being orphaned and relegated to the care of public institutions, of her many attempts to escape, of her initiation into petty crime, and of ending up in a reform school. It is not a paradox to say that of the two processes we see at work in his films – starting with Hitchcock and introducing elements of Renoir, or starting with a Renoirian series of character studies and using great technical virtuosity – it is in the first that Truffaut is most clearly revealed. 'In adapting books describing a milieu other than my own, I end up saying things I daren't say in my original scenarios. In *Baisers Volés*, for example, I had to constantly cover my tracks, camouflage myself, and transpose so that I wouldn't be too recognisable. In short, I wore a mask. In *La Mariée* or *La Sirène,* on the contrary, the mask existed *a priori,* and behind borrowed characters I felt freer to express my own personality.' Some of the best moments of the film are precisely those slack periods, which have always been Truffaut's speciality, when the characters momentarily relax and talk of themselves. A good example is the firelit scene in the country house at Aix, with its confidences and feeling of communion.

Double identity recurs frequently in Truffaut's films: Charlie the bar-room pianist turns out to be Edouard the concert pianist; Julie, the bride in white, becomes an avenging angel; in *Fahren-*

La Sirène du Mississippi: *(top) the detective (Michel Bouquet) on the trail; (bottom) Louis and Comolli.*

heit 451 Linda and Clarisse are opposite poles of Truffaut's universe; and now another Julie playing opposite roles, the angel and the demon, black and white. Julie/Marion is another in the line of dominating, obsessing women who are stronger and more confident than the men they hypnotise. The woman manipulates the situation and the man. In her 'unworthiness', Marion takes the concept a stage further than it had been taken previously. She is, at least in her original conception, the *femme fatale,* who enchants and lures to his doom the worthy and deserving male. 'What seduced me when I read *La Sirène du Mississippi* was that William Irish had treated in it a subject traditional in the pre-war cinema: it's *The Devil is a Woman, The Blue Angel, La Chienne, Nana.* This theme of the vamp, of the *femme fatale,* subjugating an honest man to the point of making a rag-doll out of him, had been treated by all the cineastes I admire. I said to myself that I must, too . . . and now, too late, I realise I can't. The scene where the baron in *Nana* gets down on hands and knees and begs like a dog for the *marrons glacés,* and the one where Emil Jannings crows like a rooster in *The Blue Angel,* these are scenes I admire, but I'm just not capable of filming them. Perhaps that's one of the reasons I transposed *La Sirène* into the present: nowadays, things don't happen that way. That sort of woman isn't a tramp any longer, she's something much more comprehensible, and her victim is no longer entirely a victim. The black and white have become shades of grey. So despite myself, I weakened the contrast between the characters, at the risk of de-dramatising the subject a little.'

Thus instead of showing a cruelly calculating Julie, Truffaut almost justifies her; though we see her indifferent to the death of her bird, for instance, the Julie of the book strangled it. Where Louis in the book was naïve and credulous, he is here aware of what is happening to him, and accepts it. When he kills the detective, instead of it being a further sign of feebleness and of subjection, it becomes an affirmation of his commitment to Marion, a deliberate act of passion and devotion.

As Truffaut foresaw, the result is de-dramatisa-

La Sirène du Mississippi: *(top) Comolli gets too close; (bottom) Comolli and Marion: Louis has committed himself.*

tion: most of the violence, both physical and moral, is gone from the film version, as is the sense of an implacable fatality. We know why Louis and Marion are what they are, and do what they do. The humanising influence of Renoir is the essential one. 'To start with, I accept the novelettish trappings, but then I set off at a tangent. I require people to behave normally in a totally abnormal situation. Doubtless I do this because I identify with my characters. When Louis catches up with Julie, he whips out his revolver and says to her "I've come to kill you". But already I feel that if it was me, I wouldn't know what to do with a revolver; so he goes on to say "There's nothing magic about a revolver: I can't pull the trigger".'

Given the extent of Renoir's influence on Truffaut, and given his almost symbolic significance in Truffaut's mind, it is not too surprising that this adaptation of a murder story should be dedicated to him. The theme, after all, started off as a parallel to *La Chienne*. One rather unfortunate result is the introductory sequence, which, on the grounds of recounting a moment in the history of the island, borrows a sequence from Renoir's *La Marseillaise*. It provides a bewildering and unpromising opening, and suggests that as in *Tirez sur le pianiste* Truffaut's detailed acquaintance with the cinema momentarily submerged his desire to produce spectacles for the general public, resulting in certain scenes which can only really appeal to initiates. The film mentioned at Aix is *Arizona Jim,* not a real film but one of the names invented by Monsieur Lange in Renoir's *Le Crime de Monsieur Lange*. The idea for the ending, with the couple setting off into the snow towards the Swiss frontier, was borrowed from *La Grande Illusion*.

There are other notations of lesser importance, such as the references to favourite authors: we have a Monorail Hotel, named after an Audiberti novel Truffaut would like to adapt, and appropriately situated in Jacques Audiberti Square; and we have another of Balzac's books, 'La Peau de Chagrin', being read by Louis in the mountain hut. The comments on the book are calculated to refer equally to *La Sirène*. When Louis collapses in the aeroplane on his way to France, he is transported to the Clinique Heurtebise: Heurtebise was the chauffeur in Cocteau's *Orphée* who conducted Orpheus into the Underworld. Entering the clinic, Louis is entering on the infernal period of his existence, in search of his own Eurydice; the depth of his devotion conquers death. Amongst other quotations, it is worthwhile mentioning Nicholas Ray's *Johnny Guitar* which had an enormous influence on Truffaut in a variety of ways: the quality of the colour, the realism, and Ray's use of a traditional genre (the western) to communicate personal themes. Finally, the name of the detective, Comolli, is borrowed from the editor of Cahiers du Cinéma.

Truffaut introduced more personal material into *La Sirène du Mississippi* than he had into his previous adaptation of a William Irish novel, *La Mariée était en noir*. The book is set in nineteenth-century New Orleans. Truffaut's principal motive in transposing it to the present day was his desire to avoid becoming involved in a historical drama. The preparation of costumes and dialogue would have been even more time-consuming and costly than they already were. At about 800 million francs, this was the most expensive film he had yet undertaken, outstripping even *Fahrenheit 451,* which had required elaborate décors not needed here. Moreover, the greater degree of formal preparation would have hindered his tendency to improvise dialogue and even whole scenes at the last moment. The change from New Orleans to Réunion was similarly motivated. Making the film in America would have meant making it in English, and his unpleasant memories of *Fahrenheit 451* were due at least partly to language difficulties. The atmosphere of authenticity he manages to create in his characterisation depends largely on the informal and even highly colloquial nature of dialogue. 'I write them each evening for the next day, and like to manipulate even at the last moment. In *La Sirène du Mississippi* I was even reluctant to write them down. I dictated them, to avoid anything too literary. I could never have done this in English. I give myself till 1972 to learn English, because *La Sirène* is one of the last high-budget films to be made without an English version. It's madness in a production costing 800 million.'

The film was first screened publicly on 18 June 1969, and was only moderately successful. Although its exclusive run lasted almost as long as that of *Baisers Volés*, it attracted barely half as many spectators, though it cost several times as much. Subsequently it disappeared almost com-

pletely from the cinemas, over-shadowed by the films which came before and after it – *Baisers Volés* and *L'Enfant Sauvage*. Critics were divided into a large disappointed group and, on the other hand, its extravagant supporters.

Truffaut himself conceded that something must have gone wrong: 'Perhaps what I had tried to do before in *Tirez sur le pianiste* and *La Mariée était en noir* – combine an adventure story and a love story – worked less well here. If I met from time to time someone who really liked it . . . but

La Sirène du Mississippi: *Louis listening to the siren song: beauty and wealth may eradicate the past.*

as those who don't like it constitute 95%, I have to admit something went wrong. I'm not stubborn, I don't play the misunderstood poet. I think it must have been caused by a phenomenon common enough when you start from a meaty book: you admire the construction, retain the chronology, and reject what you think irrelevant (so as to stay within the two hours). But in what you reject there were undoubtedly things necessary to substantiate the episodes you included. In an original scenario you're in greater control from beginning to end. In an adaptation, even when you're steeped in the book itself, you have trouble distinguishing the relative importance of the minor scenes –

especially as here, in an account of a steady degradation.'

The principal criticism was that the film lacked vitality or excitement while purporting to be an adventure story. The music also was criticised, and it can seem crude and over-insistent, though it is composed by the musician who worked on *Baisers Volés* and was later to work on *Domicile Conjugal*. It does seem inappropriate to accompany the detective with the same mock-sinister plucked bass as accompanies the genuinely mock-sinister characters in those two films.

Lastly, the choice of actors was criticised, and Truffaut was finally forced to admit doubts, if only on the grounds that he hadn't succeeded in imposing these actors on the public. Talking of *Domicile Conjugal*, he says that he has always filmed the same character, and has always asked the person playing that character to act like

Léaud: 'I think that Léaud is even the real character behind Louis in *La Sirène*. Probably, the public would have accepted more willingly from him what it refused from Belmondo, whom it associated with an idea of virility as Catherine Deneuve is associated with sweetness.' Belmondo's roles in *A bout de souffle* and *Pierrot le fou* influenced Truffaut's choice, and Louis can seem an uneasy blend of Antoine Doinel and Pierrot. Just as *La Sirène* is in a way a remake of *Tirez sur le pianiste*, so *Pierrot le fou* was a sort of remake of *A bout de souffle,* and all four have the identical theme: a comfortably established man becomes obsessed with a woman and quits his bourgeois surroundings to follow her; the couple become involved in a sort of fringe life in an idyllic setting until reality intrudes in the form of money and gangsters; the woman betrays the man and the result is death.

L'Enfant Sauvage

The idea of making a film on this subject had first occurred to Truffaut in 1966 when he read a review in Le Monde of Lucien Malson's book 'Les Enfants Sauvages,' examining all known cases of children who had grown up in a wild state, deprived of any real human contact. It's easy to see why the theme appealed to him so immediately: referring to Antoine Doinel, or on the rare occasions when he speaks of his own childhood, Truffaut invariably underlines the lack of affection, the feeling of being unwanted and even rejected by his parents. He had called his first film 'a study in isolation', and said Antoine was not so much maltreated as simply not treated at all. Here this same experience was treated scientifically – his own childhood in mythical terms. Lucien Malson echoes Truffaut's own childhood when he writes: 'If food, light, heat – and also affection – should happen to be lacking, natural development is

L'Enfant Sauvage: *the wild child (Jean-Pierre Cargol) is captured by the civilised dog.*

L'Enfant Sauvage *(above): the alter ego of Antoine Doinel: pure vulnerability.*

of any social context.'

Truffaut's choice of Victor de l'Aveyron out of the 52 cases described in Malson's book is also readily explicable. Victor, when discovered, was about eleven or twelve years old. Antoine in *Les Quatre Cents Coups* is aged 12 or 13, and the age is particularly significant in Truffaut's own life. But there were other reasons: this was the first fully documented case of such a wild boy; and the cool, rational style of an Itard narration particularly appealed to him. Moreover, in the person of Dr Itard, Truffaut no doubt saw a welcome opportunity to acquit himself of his debt to his own rescuer, André Bazin.

He lived with the project for three years, hesitating only because of the considerable technical problems involved in reconstituting a historical episode and in finding a child capable of rendering the role. The scene in which Itard unjustly punishes Victor finally decided him that the film must be made: he was fascinated by the moral intensity of such a situation in much the same way he had been fascinated by the strong situ-

L'Enfant Sauvage *(below): protected by the older man from contempt and curiosity of rural France for an obviously inferior being.*

seriously perturbed . . . There is no "human nature" in the sense that there are "chemical natures" which can be conclusively defined by their properties. Man, however, in society, realises certain potentials which distinguish him incontestably from other higher animals . . . Man deprived of contact with other men can be nothing but a monster . . . "Wild boys" – those deprived too soon by chance or design of the human educational environment – are simple cases of deformity . . . We have to realise that men are not men, deprived

ations in American films and novels. With *La Sirène du Mississippi* finished, he and Jean Gruault began to elaborate a scenario divided roughly into two – the capture, and the subsequent re-education – but he soon realised that it would be necessary to relegate the first to the status of a mere prologue if he was to deal adequately with the second. The principal problem was to transform into dramatic terms the two reports written by Itard, the first in 1801 for the Academy of Medicine, and the second in 1806 at the request of a government minister. 'To extract from these two texts a scenario, we imagined that Dr Itard, instead of writing these reports, kept a daily journal, which gave the film the feel of a chronicle and preserved the author's style, at once scientific, philosophical, moralistic, humanistic, and also by turns lyrical and familiar. I remained faithful to the reports . . . and re-read them repeatedly during the shooting of the film in order to remind myself of some idea or other, or simply to immerse myself thoroughly in the incident.'

Given this close adherence to the facts, the few occasions on which he distorts them are all the

L'Enfant Sauvage: *rescued from a jeering crowd by Mme Guerin (Françoise Seigner) and Doctor Jean Itard (François Truffaut).*

more interesting. First, concerning the doctor himself: Itard actually came into the narrative considerably later than the film suggests, but the pruning of the early sections results in a more unified film. For the same reason, Mme Guérin's husband and daughter have been excluded, leaving only three prominent characters: Victor and the

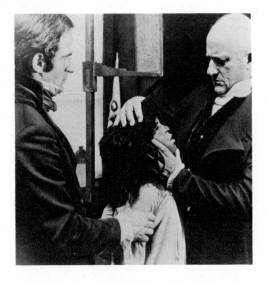

L'Enfant Sauvage: *a proper subject of enquiry for Itard and Pinel (Jean Dasté).*

two people who represent the twin poles of his re-education, the emotional and the intellectual.

Itard was plagued by rather more doubts about the validity of his methods, and was more pessimistic about eventual success, than the film suggests. There are two other striking changes. The shedding of Victor's first tears has been displaced. In Itard's account, Victor has an uncontrollable fear of heights, which was used to vanquish his increasingly frequent epileptic fits. When one such crisis threatens, Itard holds Victor

out of a fourth-floor window, with devastating effects, including his first tears. This incident would have shown Itard in a harsher light than does the film, though Truffaut doesn't hesitate to present him as relentless and capable of repressing sympathy if the occasion warrants. But probably it was not included because it would have distorted the nature of those first tears: their function as an expression of fear, humiliation or defeat would have overshadowed the fact that they were also and fundamentally a sign of increased emotional sensitivity.

Secondly, although Victor is reported to have fled several times from captivity, the circumstances were never those of the film, and more important, he never came back of his own accord. When recaptured, however, he would show great joy at being reunited with Mme Guérin, though his affection for Dr Itard was naturally more qualified. In the film, his inability to live in the forest after being acquainted with civilisation is also exaggerated. The changes are made for dramatic reasons.

Many other sections of the report must have tempted Truffaut, but apart from the running time of the average film, certain of these incidents would have presented insuperable practical problems. Since it was summer, he could not show Victor's winter satisfactions, such as rolling in the snow; it would have been difficult to show Victor's insensitivity to boiling water or to flaming coals; his education in colour sensitivity would have been hard to convey in a black and white film; but in particular he excludes all mention of Victor's awakening to sexual sensations. This material might have assumed a disproportionate importance, at least in spectators' minds.

Apart from using Itard's accounts, Truffaut did not document himself to any great extent, though he did read a few works on the deaf and dumb. 'I'm always afraid that too much documentation will make me give up a project, because I come to realise that the subject is too vast: I like to restrict my aims right from the start. I already had to limit the film to an hour and a half, when obviously with such a subject you could add details until it was at least three hours long. I

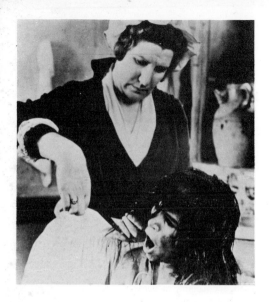

L'Enfant Sauvage: *the humiliations of civilised appearance: Mme Guerin wields the scissors.*

also rejected the idea of calling in technical advice on the medical aspects, in case it ruled out certain things I had set my heart on. I merely consulted a few people, often during shooting; for example we had to use tuning forks, and I wanted it to seem authentic, so I invited an ear specialist to dinner and he gave me a few ideas. Starting from there, I managed to improvise two little scenes on the education of the ear that I couldn't otherwise have imagined. But I didn't want the technical advice to be systematic.

'Before shooting I had several medical films on autistic children projected for me, and I noticed a wide range of behaviour in them. Certain of them were very mild, docile, and slow, and did something insistent like tapping on the table all day; others are quite frenetic; some, when they survey their surroundings, do so like an animal; others never focus on anything. So I thought I

had every right to invent.'

Despite this element of invention, the effect is that of a documentary. Before *Les Quatre Cents Coups*, Truffaut was determined that he would never resign himself to the documentary style: he wanted to create 'acted' films. He refers to Hitchcock, who as he grew older began to lose interest in the novel, and turned to reading memoirs. Whatever the reason, Truffaut's style has changed: there are more explanatory scenes than usual, each episode and each exercise being meticulously prepared. 'It was absolutely necessary that from the beginning of each exercise the public should realise what Dr Itard wanted of the child, so as to follow his progress without losing interest; I made sure of this by adding Itard's voice off, reading comments from his diary.' At the same time, he distinguishes between this scruple for comprehensibility and 'a phoney reporting style: the most ridiculous way of approaching this film would have been to aim at authenticity through imitating reporting techniques. It's a film where everything is re-created, and the re-creation is obviously more poetic than scientific.'

Which is another way of saying that it is a poetic documentary – a factual narrative, in which the author has licence. Truffaut likens it to science fiction. His problems were similar to those of *Fahrenheit 451*, which like this film, deals with cultural deprivation. In *Les Quatre Cents Coups* the deprivation had been emotional. It has been said that *L'Enfant Sauvage* contradicts all his previous films: they had taken an already sensitive person and shown him rejecting society's values, while this film takes an ignorant person and shows him being led towards those values. But it is also another case of an individual in hostile surroundings (whether over- or under-civilised) asserting personal values which are equally absent from the forest and from modern society. Antoine Doinel at the end of *Les Quatre Cents Coups* has freed himself from early repressions, and can begin to develop his own potential. Itard provides such a possibility for Victor. Truffaut has always advocated 'true' civilisation, not to be identified with society. *Fahrenheit 451* showed them to be clearly opposed.

L'Enfant Sauvage: *Itard and his pupil.*

Itard does not offer Victor a place in Parisian society (which, so far as it appears in the film is gently mocked). He tries to introduce him to the worlds of literacy and the imagination, more real to Truffaut than the society in which they are created. *L'Enfant Sauvage* could be said to summarise *Les Quatre Cents Coups* and *Fahrenheit 451*. Victor himself implicitly accepts this thesis when, at the end, he returns. The scenario ends on this note of positive achievement, when it might just as well have included some comment on the subsequent twenty-five years, comparatively devóid of progress. The film is a committed interpretation. Justifying the mild optimism of the ending, Truffaut said that he generally arranged ambiguous or pessimistic ends, 'so as not to betray life, which is not exactly hilarious. But when you have a theme you believe in, you can't be entirely pessimistic. *L'Enfant Sauvage* was a little like

Fahrenheit 451, which also ends on a hopeful note. Even if the child hasn't managed to speak, a certain basic communication has been established . . . Into my decision to make the film went a degree of irritation at something much spoken of lately – the inability to communicate: "We use the same words, but we don't understand each other." I think this idea has been made too much of, notably by Antonioni. What pleases me in *L'Enfant Sauvage* is that these recent ideas are kept in the background and we focus on the essential: it's tremendous to be able to make yourself understood, it's tremendous to stand upright, it's tremendous to walk in shoes . . . Elementary? That doesn't worry me.'

There were two principal characters. For the boy, Truffaut had two possibilities in mind: either an extremely sophisticated boy, or one similar to Léaud and the *Mistons*. He had always thought, from photographs, that Nureyev would make a good 'wild man', so began to look among children in dancing classes at the Opéra. They proved too docile, so he sent an assistant to southern towns looking for someone resembling the *Mistons*. She checked over 2,500 children, in Nîmes, Marseille, and Arles; and in a Montpellier street noticed and photographed a gypsy boy called Jean-Pierre Cargol whom Truffaut finally chose. More detailed psychological tests than is usual with child actors were carried out; the film was eventually shown to have been of considerable benefit to the boy.

The choice of an actor for the doctor's role caused even more trouble. Truffaut first ran through the lists of cinema, theatre and TV actors, though it seemed to him that often their fictional roles and the image of them the public already had would interfere with the documentary aspect. He therefore hunted among journalists and his friends for someone unknown to the public. Finally, since the wild boy was deaf and dumb, and needed to be directed *within* the film it seemed to Truffaut that he should play both roles, director and doctor. By the end of the third day he was thoroughly at ease. 'I don't know if I was right to do it, or if I'm a good actor, but I don't regret

L'Enfant Sauvage: *Le Gai Savoir at the hands of Doctor Itard.*

my decision. I feel that if I'd entrusted this role to an actor, *L'Enfant Sauvage* would have been, for me, the least satisfying of my films because my job would have been purely technical . . . The impression I retain of this experience is not of having played a part, but rather of having directed the film from in front of the camera instead of behind it.'

It was Truffaut's second film inspired directly by his own youth, from which he had been rescued by Bazin, the first being *Les Quatre Cents Coups,* which was dedicated to Bazin. In *L'Enfant Sauvage,* a further wild boy acted it out, Truffaut himself plays the rescuer, and the film is dedicated to Léaud, who had been the Truffaut-figure in the earlier film. Truffaut has in a very concrete sense been the rescuer of these two, establishing them in a career just as Bazin had done for him, and thus indirectly repaid his debt to Bazin. The film crew offered an 8 mm camera to Jean-Pierre Cargol at the end of shooting, whereupon he announced that he would become 'the first gypsy film director'.

The sort of indication Truffaut gives to his actors is more readily apparent here than in most of his films. One rule he imposed on himself was 'no smiling' – the same rule he had imposed on Léaud in *Les Quatre Cents Coups,* on Charlie in *Pianiste,* on Jeanne Moreau in *La Mariée* to the same end: to attain a certain 'gravity', that same quality which had guided his choice of Belmondo for *La Sirène.* 'I never smile during the film. It's a decision I took beforehand, and which justified itself all the more because I proved *incapable* of smiling. I *can* smile, as now during an interview, but never while working. It didn't worry me, because I wanted Itard to be like that, absorbed in his work, and even a little egocentric, for he can be tough with the child.' The rule also acted as a sort of self-defence against the label *'Truffaut la tendresse'* which critics had applied to his films, and which seemed to him even more inappropriate than most labels.

Truffaut would specify for the boy certain animals as an indication of what he wanted: glancing around 'like a dog', or tossing his head 'like a horse'. Or to express astonishment, Truffaut mimed Harpo Marx's enormous eyes. One difficulty was the violence. Despite his background, Jean-Pierre was a happy and well-balanced child, and had trouble with the nose-bleeding and the thrashing about on the floor. For this reason, these scenes were kept short, ending before their artificiality became too apparent. This didn't worry Truffaut too much, because it had never been his intention to emphasise horror and violence. The most difficult scenes of all to fake were the ones in which the dogs hunt and seize Victor: it's a little too obvious that the good-natured dogs are having their mouths held and twisted by Victor, and are feeling rather affronted.

In general, where another director might have seized the opportunity of Victor's animal scenes to include a little gruesome 'realism', Truffaut worked in the direction of understatement. The result is a remarkable austerity. Feeling the emotional potential of the situation sufficient to hold attention without artificial aids, he applied his favourite maxim: the treatment should be in inverse proportion to the emotional charge. In this respect, the film is closer in feel to those of Bresson's than are any of his other films. Even the commentary is spoken in a rapid, subdued, unemotional voice.

It is the 'purest' of his films, in the sense that

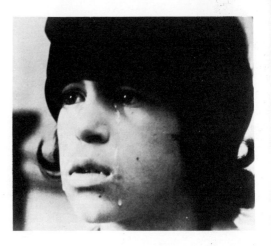

L'Enfant Sauvage: *the wild child finds out about punishment.*

he allows himself no digressions from the simple linear narrative, and few if any private jokes. In *Baisers Volés* the choice of incidents can seem arbitrary, or at least not logically justifiable, and the background (like that of other of his films) is packed with details which to him and to those with his cultural background have a hidden significance. *L'Enfant Sauvage* consists solely of 'necessary' scenes. It is worth remarking, however, that the choice of Jean Dasté for the part of Pinel links the film with Jean Vigo's *Zéro de conduite,* in which he played the popular young teacher, and therefore with *Les Quatre Cents Coups* which Vigo's film so markedly influenced. The phrase *'Comme cette eau est fraîche'*, spoken by Itard to profit from Victor's interest in the vowel 'o' was introduced by Truffaut: the words and the intonation are straight out of Marcel Carné's *Les Visiteurs du soir*, but this might have been an unconscious echo.

There are no traces of virtuosity, and the only technique which attracts attention is the irising in and out. Recalling the early days of the cinema, it gives the film a dated feel. This impression is reinforced by the fact that the visual half of the

L'Enfant Sauvage: *halting progress.*

sound–image partnership constantly predominates, so that at times it feels like a silent film, to which a commentary has been added. This is partly due to Victor's inability to speak, but also to a deliberate attempt on Truffaut's part, which we have already noted in *Baisers Volés,* to recapture some of the effects of the early cinema which had tended to disappear with the advent of sound. I know it's ridiculous to make films today in the way they were made in 1935, but those films held a secret, deriving from the fact that their

directors had begun in the days of silent films. I feel that with their death, something of value is disappearing. That's why in my recent films I've tried to link up with some of their techniques, and with the discipline which a purely visual medium imposes.'

The introduction is totally devoid of dialogue: the first sightings, the capture, the exhibition of the boy before the crowds, his passage from one institution to another, are developed purely visually, the soundtrack occupied predominantly by scuffling, barking, the muffled shouts of the hunters, the subdued babble of the crowd. There is no dialogue in the first fifteen minutes, and much of the rest depends either on commentary or on Vivaldi's invigorating music, which conveys a sense of exhilaration at each of the boy's achievements. We also find in this film the visual opposition between the forest and the closed institutions; and, finally, Dr Itard's house, set in parkland, which represents an attempt to balance the two forces. Some of the most striking parts of the film show Victor distracted, during his lessons, by windows opening onto park and forest, or perhaps, reminded of his earlier habitat by what he is drinking, show him framed against an open window with trees beyond. Descriptions of such scenes, together with comments on their significance, were already present in Itard's reports. The opposition of liberty and restriction is reflected in the pans and tracking shots in the forest, contrasting with the camera's immobility in interiors.

Inevitably, all this reminds us of the city/countryside opposition in Truffaut's earlier films, but with the difference that in *L'Enfant Sauvage,* nature is for the first time presented as inadequate, instead of simply unattainable. It seemed to some that he was betraying previous films in which he had portrayed individuals striving to reach out to the liberating and reconciling forces of nature. Itard himself had specifically been setting out to refute such a view of nature. It seems to some that the child had been free and following his natural bent in the forest, whereas all that Itard had done was thwart, constrain, and inflict needless suffering on a helpless child. There are two ways

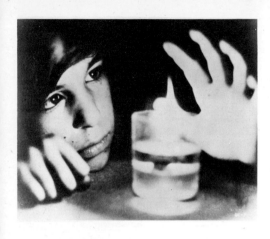

L'Enfant Sauvage: *learning to emote*

of answering such reproaches: first, within the context of Truffaut's system of symbols, it is relevant to remember that he had just made *La Sirène du Mississippi*, which is overtly romantic in that the ideals and dreams associated with the countryside are allowed to assert themselves comparatively without restraint. His films tend to alternate between such idealism and the more realistic films, such as *La Peau Douce* and *Baisers Volés*, where the problems and complexities of existence prevent the realisation of such ideals. After *La Sirène,* he seems to have felt a need for a more realistic and classical approach, where

ideals are tempered by an appreciation of the values of culture, self-control and civilisation. But for once, the irruption of reality doesn't entirely destroy the dream: *L'Enfant Sauvage* is as close as Truffaut has ever come to achieving the difficult balance of ideal and real. Whenever in his films one or other of the two has dominated, the result has been disastrous for the characters involved.

The personal significance of the theme for Truffaut explains his violent reaction to such criticism: 'There will always be people who say of the wild boy that he was better off in the forest since Itard never managed to teach him to speak. This is not true: he had led a miserable existence in the forest, as could be seen from the multiple scars on his body, for he wasn't suited to such a life. As for the pessimistic judgment you can make on the outcome of the film – "he was no longer an animal, but he wasn't a man" – I would reply that progress had been made: the banal and derisory existence which he subsequently led till his death at the age of forty was nevertheless better than that he had led in the forest. For me, there's no doubt about that.' Since the film represents a distant transposition of his own life, to admit that the child should have been left in the forest would be equivalent for Truffaut to saying that *he* should have been left to a life of petty crime, and that André Bazin was wrong to take such an interest in him. *L'Enfant Sauvage* is a further attempt on Truffaut's part to balance the account between the individual and society, between liberty and responsibility: how much freedom can or must one sacrifice to social processes in pursuit of personal fulfilment?

Domicile Conjugal

At the time of *Baisers Volés*, Henri Langlois, to whom it was dedicated, had remarked to Truffaut that it would be absolutely necessary to show the world something of Antoine's married life. It was from this suggestion that *Domicile Conjugal* grew; hence, perhaps, the fact that it does not adopt any new form or propose any new blend of elements, but repeats a formula which, in theme, treatment, and even quite small detail, had already proved effective. It is thus the least experimental of all his films. This is a pity, since Truffaut has aptly likened his own talent to the job he allots to Léaud in the film: 'The thing is to organise blends, like Antoine with his flower-tinting. And success is by no means necessary to justify the experiment. Films where there is no experimental side are less interesting to make, and there is less room for failure.'

His new film was conceived and executed even more rapidly than *La Peau Douce* or *Baisers Volés*. Shooting was begun on 21 January 1970 and finished in the first days of March. The scenario started, as had that of *Baisers Volés*, as a series of situations and gags, around each of which a scene was subsequently built; and the overall story-line was also patterned on *Baisers Volés* so as to provide a framework capable of accommodating anything. Nevertheless there is a more logical progression underlying *Domicile Conjugal* – marriage, expectant mother, baby, affair, and return to the fold – than in the earlier film. The incidents to be fitted into this framework were comic. Satisfied with the balance in *Baisers Volés* between comic and bitter, he intended to try to repeat it; but irritated by further talk of 'half-tones' in his work, he decided to push both to extremes. 'I asked Claude de Givray and Bernard

Revon to make it even more of a comedy, perhaps even a burlesque, accepting the horrible risk of people simply not laughing at it. Which allowed us to be extremely harsh in the dispute scenes, the more so because they were now married.'

Marriage has not changed Antoine: it has not reconciled him with society. His only contact with Big Business is through sailing boats on a model harbour. He is still playing. But he is as solemn in his approach to his 'floral art' as he was towards his job as a detective in *Baisers Volés*. Still self-centred, he is far from being wholly admirable. In his preface to the published scenarios, Truffaut describes him as 'a cunning character; he has charm, and knows how to use it; he lies a lot, and dissimulates a lot more; he asks for more love than he himself has to give; he's by no means man in general, but one particular man.'

He is still as he was in *L'Amour à vingt ans*, an adolescent with adolescent dreams, that have

Domicile Conjugal: *Antoine (Jean-Pierre Léaud) and Christine (Claude Jade).*

only been momentarily diverted by the lesson Delphine Seyrig taught him in *Baisers Volés*. His first job is carefully chosen to comment on his situation and personality. Flower-tinting, as an occupation, seems to date from the pre-war years. This fits in with the anachronistic feel of Antoine's character; Truffaut is looking back to his own childhood which itself was turned towards the past. The job also echoes the recalcitrant asocial element in his character: we see all the flowers

Domicile Conjugal: *Christine, Antoine and a tender surprise.*

obediently changing colour, except one: 'There's always one that stays the same, I don't know why.' That one's Antoine, who doesn't deliberately rebel against the rules by which everyone else is living, but seems simply not to know them. 'He doesn't contest society, he'd even like to become an intrinsic part of it, provided that didn't assume an unpleasant form. He'd like, basically, to be like everyone else.' A certain vague social awareness has begun to show through the apolitical front Truffaut has previously endowed him with. The prostitute makes some slighting remarks about the government's competence and talks with him of the necessity of paying some attention to political matters; this may be a direct result of

the 'Affaire Langlois' and the May riots, but Antoine has always been anti-authoritarian.

His diverse and undirected character is expressed in the mixtures of colour in his work. Likening him to the tenor's wife, who is never on time, the old man says 'He's always in a furious rage with his wife, because she's like you with your flowers – red, blue, green, yellow, ah ah ah . . .' Expressing this opposition between a clockwork mentality and a blurred awareness of time passing in terms reminiscent of Jean-Paul Sartre's 'La Nausée', Christine says 'Well, I'm not like you: I don't like haziness, I don't like vagueness, I don't like what's equivocal, I don't like ambiguity. Me, I like what's clear cut.' She incarnates precisely the sort of bourgeois characteristics described in 'La Nausée': essentially serious, prim and precise, she has become more so with marriage, which for her has once and for all defined their future existence. Antoine has no such precise idea of the future; his adolescent dreams are already beginning to reassert themselves and this is delicately suggested by his sudden devotion to the creation of an 'absolute red'. This reminds us of the absolute he had sought in the past films; and the minor catastrophe that results from his

Domicile Conjugal *(below): Antoine, Christine and Alphonse/Ghislain.*

experiments reflects in a slightly farcical form the disillusion resulting from such obsessions at least twice before. Similarly, red flowers betray his romance to Christine, by opening inconveniently and delivering their messages to the wrong person.

Antoine has married Christine largely because she has the intimate convictions and certainties he lacks. It is also because of her happy family background, for as far back as *L'Amour à vingt ans* he is looking for a family into which he can integrate himself 'I don't fall in love with only a girl, I fall for the whole family: father, mother . . . I like girls who have nice parents . . . I adore other people's parents, that's about the size of it.'

As we have come to expect, his vague romanticism crystallises around a woman. This time she is Japanese, 'another continent' like Marion in *La Sirène*, as exotic and prestigious as Nicole in Pierre Lachenay's Lisbon encounter, as Delphine Seyrig in *Baisers Volés,* or as Jeanne Moreau in her two films. Kyoko takes the initiative in exactly the same way, manipulating him into her flat and the flatmate out of it. She appeals to that side of Antoine's nature not satisfied by the sensible domesticity of Christine. So he cedes, and we find him reading a book on Japanese women, in bed beside Christine, reading one on Nureyev (who is her dream in much the same way as Kyoko is Antoine's). Thinking of *L'Enfant Sauvage,* Truffaut said Nureyev would make a fine 'wild man': his Tartar birth provides a nice analogy for Antoine's and Truffaut's own wild youth, and he has dominated this 'savage' in himself, using it to create a work of art as Truffaut did in making his first film, or as Antoine hopes to in writing a novel. In fact, in marrying Antoine, Christine has been seeking to satisfy these very cravings, bringing an element of danger and unpredictability into her life.

Their respective dreams conflict, and disaster ensues. The scenes of disruption between Antoine and Christine are Truffaut's cruellest since *La Peau Douce.* The parallels between the two films are striking, but instead of the bitter, realistic treatment of the former film, the treatment of *Domicile Conjugal* is almost farcical. In both, a

Domicile Conjugal: *Antoine and Kyoko (Mlle Miroko); an Oriental version of Truffaut's inscrutable woman.*

private dream is painfully destroyed. Antoine acts as weakly and indecisively as Pierre Lachenay, shuttling back and forth between the two women, unable to make a definitive choice because it will mean denying part of himself. It is clear that he hadn't listened to Delphine Seyrig's little homily in *Baisers Volés.* This time he recognises the truth of it.

He learns through boredom. The absolute doesn't change, and Antoine's encounters with Kyoko possess that quality of immobility and infinite repetition he had sought, but which proves rather disconcerting in reality. Minutes count double, then triple. Antoine's body protests violently at the positions it is called upon to adopt. He finds himself in the odd situation of confiding to his wife the problems he has with his mistress: a little boy fleeing to his mother when he's hurt. Significantly he calls Christine

'my little sister, my daughter, my mother . . .'
She points out she had been under the impression
he wanted a wife, and drives off. As in *Baisers
Volés*, he is totally abandoned, disengaged from
both wife and mistress. He turns to a refuge of
his not so distant youth, prostitutes; and as he
leaves them, he mutters, 'Yes, it's the end of the
month, the end of all ends, the end of the line.
I detest everything that ends, everything that fades
away . . . [in a whisper] . . . it's the end of the
film.'

Convinced at last – again – of the error of his
ways, Antoine breaks with Kyoko and returns
to Christine. The phone call from the restaurant
repeats the phrases of the reconciliation of Louis
and Marion in *La Sirène du Mississippi*. And in
the final scene, we see the young couple involved
in the same ritual their neighbours have several
times performed before our eyes: the wild man
has, at least in one sense, become civilised. When
the tenor's wife looks on fondly and says 'Now
they really love one another', we feel much as
Antoine had at the end of *Baisers Volés*: we
agree, but we feel a little disconcerted.

Perhaps our discomfort arises partly from the
fact that this is a bitter, or at least ambiguous,
ending to a supposedly comic film: we had
thought it was all in good fun. Truffaut has once
again placed fidelity to experience above formal
neatness, or preserving unity of tone. Saying that
he wished to keep the ending as far as possible
from moralising, Truffaut added 'But the singer
next door serves to remind us of this: whether
you're a tenor, or Antoine himself, or the chap on
the corner, the *Domicile Conjugal* is never entirely
a place of rest and relaxation.'

The themes and treatment are almost identical
to those of *Baisers Volés*, and we have innumerable minor cross-references. There is a similarly
enigmatic and vaguely menacing character, whose
presence is revealed to be innocent. Moreover, he
relates to the underlying theme of absolutes as
did Christine's admirer in *Baisers Volés*: appearing
on TV, he gives an imitation of Delphine Seyrig
which begins as a take-off of *L'Année Dernière à
Marienbad*, but ends with the following phrases
straight out of *Baisers Volés*: 'I'm not an

Domicile Conjugal: *Antoine.*

apparition, I'm a woman, which is quite the
opposite. You say I'm exceptional, and it's true,
I'm exceptional . . .' Not surprisingly, Antoine
finds it as hard to join in Christine's laughter at
this performance as he had to agree about the
madness of her mysterious admirer at the end
of *Baisers Volés*; for these phrases contain the
lesson he was supposed to have learned in that
film, but obviously hasn't, as the next scenes show.

The forager in rubbish-bins also returns at
intervals to borrow money from Antoine. On him
centres a whole society of such eccentric,
'exceptional' figures. There is Ginette, the sexy
waitress, another of Truffaut's assertive females.
There is the man who retired to his room
twenty-five years before, never to leave it.
Truffaut has said that in including him, he had
in mind the idea that there were hundreds of such
people, cut off from society either physically or
psychologically, who were in a sense latter-day
enfants sauvages. Then there is Césarin, the owner
of the bistro, and half-a-dozen others. There are
so many such characters, bordering on the
grotesque, that Truffaut became nervous during
the preparation of the scenario that they might
conflict with one another; often conceived as
types rather than individuals, they might detract

Domicile Conjugal: *Antoine and Parisian society.*

Domicile Conjugal: *Antoine.*

from the authenticity of the film. As usual, however, his dialogue and his manner of directing tended to humanise them during the actual shooting.

It was because of this affectionate portrayal of the 'little people' of Paris (slightly sentimentalised) that *domicile conjugal* was compared to the pre-war films of René Clair. There is a likeness, but Truffaut's characters are more realistic. They are filmed in real settings, unlike Clair's. In Truffaut's films these minor characters are present for their own sake and impinge only incidentally on the narrative, whereas René Clair's scenarios are more tightly constructed.

As in *Baisers Volés,* Truffaut has tried to introduce an element of indirectness into the narrative. The first phrases of his work-notes read: 'We'll avoid an exposition in the traditional sense of the word, that's to say documentary and undramatic. We'll seek rather to get across to the public in an amusing way a) that Antoine is married; b) that his job is tinting flowers.' All such basic factors of the situation are left unstated, and have to be deduced by the spectator. Later, when Antoine leaves Christine, there is no explanation of the visiting arrangements by which he is to come back from time to time to play with or to look after Alphonse/Ghislain.

After an original moment of confusion, the spectator is forced to assume that some such arrangement exists.

The onus is on the actors to explain the situations despite the wilful deviousness of the dialogue. Together with the emphasis on character and relationships, this makes it an actor's film, in which technique is subsidiary. Comparing it to *L'Enfant Sauvage,* for which he had also done the photography, Nestor Almendros says that in *Domicile Conjugal* the camera had to be completely self-effacing, for fear of attracting attention away from the actors; the only requirement was that the film should be immediately legible. In *L'Enfant Sauvage,* ideas, atmosphere and objects all played an important part. In *Domicile Conjugal* the only *objects* of importance are the boats on the model harbour, which echo certain of the relationships, such as Antoine and Kyoko's meeting, or Antoine and Christine's quarrel.

This is apparently to be the last of the Antoine Doinel cycle, and Truffaut has published the scenarios and work-notes as a posthumous homage to his persona. It is clear in *Domicile Conjugal* that he is running out of inspiration. Ideas and themes are thin on the ground. If he was praised for applying the principle of one idea per scene, it was because the idea behind each scene was readily apparent, whereas in his earlier autobiographical films he assimilated several themes and ideas into one scene in order to concentrate abundant material into the required time-span. Here the impression is rather of bulking out scanty material by developing old references, or relying on the spectators' previously acquired involvement in Antoine's adventures. Truffaut's marriage, the birth of his children and the preparatory work on his first feature film all date from the years around 1960, the period of *Les Quatre Cents Coups*; and the novel Antoine is now writing is unmistakably linked to *Les Quatre Cents Coups*. It is to be about his youth and family life, and Christine criticises it on the grounds that 'settling old debts is no way to create a work of art'. Is she voicing Truffaut's own doubts about *Les Quatre Cents Coups*, or merely showing bourgeois distaste for a certain type of art form; or both? Whatever Truffaut's own opinion is, it has always been out of his own frustrations, inadequacies, weaknesses and temptations that he has built his films, and these *have* all been a settling of old debts, whether with society or with himself.

Announcing his intention to bury Antoine Doinel, Truffaut said 'Doinel is an asocial, not an anti-social character, and though he gets on well with everyone, he gets on badly with life itself. So I find it hard to conceive of him settling down to a steady job somewhere. That's why we're going to put a stop to the series; I'd have to go much deeper into his personality, and as that doesn't belong to me alone (or to Léaud, but to both of us) I can't see how to extend it further. I have the impression, however, that the later episodes already exist: they are *Tirez sur le pianiste, La Peau Douce*, and with due allowance for the dream-like format, *Fahrenheit 451*.' All his films with adult leads have developed the problems implicit in Antoine Doinel's situation, and in all probability

Domicile Conjugal: *Christine and Antoine: marital bliss.*

so will his future films; that is, they will develop the conflict between people for whom life is relative and those for whom it is absolute, between dream and reality, art and life, savagery and civilisation.

Credits

1955: UNE VISITE
Directed by Truffaut. Photographed by Jacques Rivette (16 mm). Edited by Alain Resnais. Shot in Jacques Doniol-Valcroze's flat.
With: Florence Doniol-Valcroze, Laura Mauri, Jean-José Richer, Francis Cognany.

1957: LES MISTONS – *The Mischief Makers*
Directed and written by Truffaut from a short story by Maurice Pons. Produced by Robert Lachenay. Photographed by Jean Maligo. Edited by Cécile Decugis. Music by Maurice Le Roux. Commentary read by Michel Francois. 26 mins. Shot in and near Nimes, August to September 1957. First shown at Tours festival, November 1957.
With: Gérard Blain, Bernadette Lafont.

1958: UNE HISTOIRE D'EAU
Directed by Truffaut and Jean-Luc Godard. Produced by Roger Fleytoux for Les Films de la Pléiade (Pierre Braunberger). Written by Truffaut. Photographed by Michel Latouche. Sound by Jacques Maumont. Edited by Godard. 18 mins. *'En hommage de Mac Sennett.'* Shot in and near Paris in Spring 1958. Released in 1961 with Jacques Demy's *Lola*.
With: Jean-Claude Brialy (*lui*), Caroline Dim (*elle*).

1959: LES QUATRE CENT COUPS – *The Four Hundred Blows*
Directed by Truffaut. Produced by Georges Charlot for Les Films du Carrosse-SEDIF. Story by Truffaut. Adaptation and dialogue by Marcel Moussy. Photographed by Henri Decäe (Dyaliscope). Sound by Jean Labussière. Art director: Bernard Evein. Edited by Marie-Joseph Yoyotte. 97 mins. Dedicated to André Bazin. Shot in Paris and Honfleur, 10 November 1958 to 5 January 1959. Released 30 June 1959.
With: Jean-Pierre Léaud (Antoine Doinel), Patrick Auffay (René Bigey), Albert Rémy (M. Doinel), Claire Maurier (Mme Doinel), Georges Flamant (M. Bigey), Yvonne Claudie (Mme Bigey), Guy Decomble (P'tite Feuille), Jeanne Moreau (woman in street with dog), Jean-Claude Brialy (man in street), Daniel Couturier, François Nocher, Richard Kanayan (children).

1960: TIREZ SUR LE PIANISTE – *Shoot the Pianist – Shoot the Piano-Player*
Directed by Truffaut. Produced by Les Films de la Pléiade. Adaptation and dialogue by Truffaut and Marcel

Moussy from 'Down There' by David Goodis (New York 1956). Photographed by Raoul Coutard (Dyaliscope). Sound by Jacques Gallois. Art director: Jacques Mély. Music by Georges Delerue. Songs by Félix Leclerc and Lucienne Vernay ('Dialogues d'amoureux') and Bobby Lapointe ('Framboise'). 80 mins. Shot in and around Paris and near Grenoble, December 1959 to January 1960. Released 15 November 1960.
With: Charles Aznavour (Charlie/Edouard Saroyan), Albert Rémy (Chico Saroyan), J. J. Aslanian (Richard Saroyan), Richard Kanayan (Fido Saroyan), Claude Mansard and Daniel Boulanger (Momo and Ernest), Marie Dubois (Lena), Nicole Berger (Thérésa), Michèle Mercier (Clarisse), Serge Davri (Plyne), Claude Heymann (Schmeel), Alex Joffe (stranger), Bobby Lapointe (singer).

1961: JULES ET JIM – *Jules and Jim*
Directed by Truffaut. Produced by Les Films du Carrosse-SEDIF. Adaptation and dialogue by Truffaut and Jean Gruault from the novel by Henri-Pierre Roché (Paris, 1953). Photographed by Raoul Coutard (Franscope). Edited by Claudine Bouché. Music by Georges Delerue. Song by Boris Bassiak ('Le Tourbillon'). Narrated by Michel Subor. 110 mins. Shot in and around Paris, Alsace and St Paul de Vence, 10 April 1961 to 3 June 1961. Première 27 January 1962.
With: Jeanne Moreau (Catherine), Oskar Werner (Jules), Henri Serre (Jim), Marie Dubois (Thérésa), Vanna Urbino (Gilberte), Boris Bassiak (Alberte), Sabine Haudepin (Sabine), Jean-Louis Richard (1st customer in café), Michel Varesano (2nd customer in café), Pierre Fabre (drunkard in café), Danielle Bassiak (Alberte's friend), Elen Bobor (Mathilde), Bernard Largemains (Merlin).

1962: ANTOINE ET COLETTE (episode in L'AMOUR A VINGT ANS – *Love at Twenty*)
Directed and written by Truffaut. Produced by Phillippe Dussart for Ulysse Productions (Pierre Rostang). Photographed by Raoul Coutard (Franscope). Edited by Claudine Bouché. Music by Georges Delerue. Other episodes directed by Renzo Rossellini, Shintaro Ishihara, Marcel Ophüls, Andrzej Wajda. Artistic supervision by Jean de Baroncelli. Linking images by Henri Cartier-Bresson, filmed by Jean Aurel. 123 mins. Truffaut's episode shot in Paris, October to December 1961. Released 22 June 1962.
With: Jean-Pierre Léaud (Antoine Doinel), Marie-France Pisier (Colette), Rosy Varte and François Darbon

(Colette's parents), Patrick Auffay (René Bigey), Jean-François Adam (Albert Tazzi).

1964: LA PEAU DOUCE – *Silken kin – Soft Skin*
Directed by Truffaut. Produced by Marcel Berbert for Les Films du Carrosse-SEDIF. Written by Truffaut and Jean-Louis Richard. Photographed by Raoul Coutard. Edited by Claudine Bouché. Music by Georges Delerue. 118 mins. Shot in Paris, Orly, Reims and Lisbon, October to December 1963. Released 10 May 1964.
With: Jean Desailly (Pierre Lachenay), Nelly Benedetti (Franca), Françoise Dorléac (Nicole), Daniel Ceccaldi (Clement), Jean Lanier (Michel), Paule Emanuele (Odile), Sabine Haudepin (Sabine), Laurence Badie (Ingrid), Gérard Poirot (Franck), Dominique Lacarrière (Pierre's secretary), Carnero (Lisbon organiser), Georges de Givray (Nicole's father), Charles Lavialle (hotel night porter), Mme Harlaut (Mme Leloix), Olivia Poli (Mme Bontemps), Catherine Duport (young girl at Reims), Philippe Dumat (cinema manager), Thérésa Renouard (cashier), Maurice Garrel (bookseller), Pierre Risch (canon), Brigitte Zhendre-Laforest.

1966: FAHRENHEIT 451
Directed by Truffaut. Produced by Lewis M. Allen for Anglo-Enterprise/Vineyard. Associate producer: Michael Delamar. Written by Truffaut and Jean-Louis Richard from the novel by Ray Bradbury (New York 1953). Additional dialogue by David Rudkin and Helen Scott. Photographed by Nicholas Roeg (Technicolor). Special effects by Charles Staffel. Sound by Norman Wanstall. Art director: Syd Caine. Costumes by Tony Walton. Edited by Thom Noble. Music by Bernard Herrmann. 110 mins. Shot in Pinewood Studios (London) and Châteauneuf-sur-Loire, 13 January to 28 April 1966. Released 16 September 1966.
With: Oskar Werner (Montag), Julie Christie (Linda and Clarisse), Cyril Cusack (fire captain), Anton Diffring (Fabian), Jeremy Spenser (man with the apple), Bee Duffell (Book-woman), Gillian Lewis (TV announcer), Ann Bell (Doris), Caroline Hunt (Helen), Anna Palk (Jackie), Roma Milne (neighbour), Arthur Cox (1st male nurse), Eric Mason (2nd male nurse), Noel Davis and David Pickering (TV announcers), Michael Mundell (storeman), Chris Williams (Black), Gillian Aldam (Judoka woman), Edward Kaye (Judoka man), Mark Lester (1st small boy), Kevin Elder (2nd small boy), Joan Francis (bar telephonist), Tom Watson (instructor). *Bookmen*: Alex Scott (The Life of Henri Brulard), Dennis Gilmore (Martian Chronicles), Fred Cox (Pride), Frank Cox (Prejudice), Michael Balfour (Machiavelli's Prince), Judith Drynan (Plato's Dialogues), David Glover (The Pickwick Papers), Yvonne Blake (The Jewish Question), John Rae (The Weir of Hermiston), Earl Younger (nephew of The Weir of Hermiston).

1968: LA MARIEE ETAIT EN NOIR – *The Bride Wore Black*
Directed by Truffaut. Produced by Marcel Berbert for Les Films du Carrosse/Artistes Associés/Dino de Laurentiis Cinematografica. Adaptation and dialogue by Truffaut and Jean-Louis Richard from the novel by William Irish (New York 1940). Photographed by Raoul Coutard and Jean Nocereau (Eastmancolor De Luxe). Sound by René Levert. Art director: Pierre Guffroy. Edited by Claudine Bouché. Music by Bernard Herrmann. 107 mins. Shot in and around Paris, and Cannes, 16 May 1967 to 24 July 1967. Released 17 April 1968.
With: Jeanne Moreau (Julie Kohler), Claude Rich (Bliss), Jean-Claude Brialy (Corey), Michel Bouquet (Coral), Michel Lonsdale (René Morane), Charles Denner (Fergus), Daniel Boulanger (Holmes), Serge Rousseau (David), Jacques Robiolles (Charlie), Luce Fabiole (Julie's mother), Sylvine Delannoy (Mme Morane), Jacqueline Rouillard (maid), Van Doude (Inspector Fabri), Paul Pavel (the mechanic), Maurice Garrel (the plaintiff), Gilles Queant (examining magistrate), Alexandra Stewart (Miss Becker), Frederique and Renaud Fontanarosa (musicians).

1968: BAISERS VOLES – *Stolen Kisses*
Directed by Truffaut. Produced by Marcel Berbert for Les Films du Carrosse/Artistes Associés. Written by Truffaut, Claude de Givray and Bernard Revon. Photographed by Denys Clerval (Eastmancolor). Sound by René Levert. Art director: Claude Pignot. Edited by Agnès Guillemot. Music by Antoine Duhamel. Song by Charles Trenet ('Que reste-t-il de nos amours?'). 91 mins. Shot in and around Paris, from 5 February 1968. Released 6 September 1968.
With: Jean-Pierre Léaud (Antoine Doinel), Claude Jade (Christine Darbon), Daniel Ceccaldi (M. Darbon), Claire Duhamel (Mme Darbon), Delphine Seyrig (Fabienne Tabard), Michel Lonsdale (M. Tabard), André Falcon (M. Vidal), Harry Max (M. Henri), Catherine Lutz (Mme Catherine), Marie-France Pisier (Colette Tazzi), Jean-François Adam (Albert Tazzi), Jacques Robiolles (writer), Serge Rousseau (Christine's admirer), Paul Pavel (Julien), Karine Jeantet.

1969: LA SIRENE DU MISSISSIPPI
Directed by Truffaut. Produced by Les Films du Carrosse/Artistes Associés. Adaptation and dialogue by Truffaut from the novel 'Waltz into Darkness' by William Irish (New York 1947). Photographed by Denys Clerval (Dyaliscope and Eastmancolor). Sound by René Levert. Art director: Claude Pignot. Edited by Agnès Guillemot. Music by Antoine Duhamel. 125 mins. Shot in Réunion, Antibes, Aix-en-Provence, Lyon and near Grenoble, December 1968 to February 1969. Released 18 June 1969.
With: Catherine Deneuve (Julie/Marion), Jean-Paul Belmondo (Louis Mahé), Michel Bouquet (Comolli), Nelly Borgeaud (Berthe Roussel), Marcel Berbert (Jardine), Martine Ferrière (landlady), Roland Thenot (Richard), Yves Drouhet.

1970: L'ENFANT SAUVAGE – *Wild Child*
Directed by Truffaut. Produced by Marcel Berbert for Les Films du Carrosse/Artistes Associés. Associate producer: Christian Lentretien. Written by Truffaut and Jean Gruault from 'Mémoire et Rapport sur Victor de

L'Aveyron' (1806) in 'Les Enfants Sauvages' by Lucien Malson. Photographed by Nestor Almendros. Sound by René Levert. Art director: Jean Mandaroux. Edited by Agnès Guillemot. Music by Vivaldi. Music director: Antoine Duhamel. 85 mins. Exteriors shot in Auvergne, 7 July 1969 to 1 September 1969. Released 26 February 1970.
With: Jean-Pierre Cargol (Victor de L'Aveyron), Truffaut (Docteur Jean Itard), Françoise Seigner (Mme Guérin), Jean Dasté (Professor Pinel), Pierre Fabre (orderly), Claude and Annie Miller (M. and Mme Lemeri), Paul Ville (Rémy), René Levert (police official), Jean Mandaroux (Itard's doctor).

1970: DOMICILE CONJUGAL – *Bed and Board*
Directed by Truffaut. Produced by Marcel Berbert for Les Films du Carrosse/Valeria Films/Fida Cinematografica. Written by Truffaut, Claude de Givray and Bernard Revon. Photographed by Nestor Almendros (Eastmancolor). Sound by René Levert. Art director: Jean Mandaroux. Edited by Agnès Guillemot. Music by Antoine Duhamel. 97 mins. Shot in and around Paris, January to March 1970. Released 1 September 1970.
With: Jean-Pierre Léaud (Antoine Doinel), Claude Jade (Christine Doinel), Mlle Hiroko (Kyoko), Daniel Ceccaldi and Claire Duhamel (M. and Mme Darbon), Barbara Laage (Monique), Jacques Jouanneau (Cesarin), Daniel Boulanger and Sylvana Blasi (tenor and wife), Claude Vega (the strangler), Pierre Fabre (office romeo), Bill Kearns (American boss), Danièle Gérard (waitress), Jacques Robiolles (sponger), Serge Rousseau, Pierre Maguelon, Marie Irakane, Rispal, Yvon Lec, Annick Asty, Guy Pirrot, Christian de Tilière, Ada Lonati

Screenplays

LES MISTONS
L'Avant-scène du Cinéma, 4, 1961.

HISTOIRE D'EAU
L'Avant-scène du Cinéma, 7, 1961.

LES QUATRE CENTS COUPS
Les Quatre Cents Coups. François Truffaut and Marcel Moussy. Gallimard, Paris 1959.
The 400 Blows: a film by François Truffaut. Translation of screenplay, edited by David Denby (including translation of article in Arts, 697, and the interview in L'Express, 24 April 1959). Grove Press Inc., New York 1969
Les Aventures d'Antoine Doinel. Francois Truffaut. Scenarios and work-notes for *Les Quatre Cent Coups, Antoine et Colette, Baisers Volés, Domicile Conjugal.*

JULES ET JIM
L'Avant scène du Cinéma, 16, June 1962. English translation by Nicholas Fry. Lorrimer, London 1968.

ANTOINE ET COLETTE
See *Les Quatre Cents Coups.*

LA PEAU DOUCE
L'Avant-scène du Cinéma, 48, May 1965.

FAHRENHEIT 451
Cahiers du Cinéma, 175–80, February–July 1966; *Journal de Fahrenheit 451*. Truffaut's diary of the making of the film. (Translated in Cahiers du Cinéma, in English, 5 and 7.)
L'Avant-scène du Cinéma, 64, October 1970 (synopsis only).

BAISERS VOLES
See *Les Quatre Cents Coups.*

L'ENFANT SAUVAGE
L'Avant-scène du Cinéma, 107, October 1970.

DOMICILE CONJUGAL
See *Les Quatre Cents Coups.*

Principal Interviews

MAGAZINES
Script, 5, April 1962.
Cahiers du Cinéma, 132, December 1962.
Realités, 220, May 1964.
Cinéma 64, 86, 87 and 89, May–October 1964.
Lui, 9, September 1964.
Cinéma 67, 112, January 1967.
Cahiers du Cinéma, 190, May 1967.
Le Nouvel Adam, 19, February 1968.
Télé-Ciné, 160, March 1970.

WEEKLIES
Arts, 720, 29 April 1969.
France-Observateur, 598, 19 October 1961.
L'Express, 883, 20 May 1968.
Le Nouvel Observateur, 200, 9 September 1968.
Le Nouvel Observateur, 277, 2 March 1970.

MISCELLANEOUS
Cinémonde, 1421, 31 October 1961.
Les Lettres Françaises, 911, 25 January 1962.
Cinémonde, 1450, 22 May 1962.
Les Lettres Françaises, 1000, 24 October 1963.
Cinémonde, 1554, 19 May 1964.
Le Figaro-Littéraire, 948, 18 June 1964.
Arts-Loisirs, 51, 14 September 1966.
Les Lettres Françaises, 1179, 20 April 1967.
Cinémonde, 1712, 26 September 1967.
Les Lettres Françaises, 1229, 11 April 1968.
Le Journal du Show-Business, 2, 36, and 68, 11 October 1968, 27 June 1969 and 20 March 1970.

Interviews by Truffaut (all appeared in Cahiers du Cinéma)

Robert Aldrich: 64 and 82.
Jacques Becker: 32.

Jules Dassin: 46 and 47.
Georges Franju: 101.
Abel Gance: 43.
Howard Hawks: 56.
Alfred Hitchcock: 44, 62, 147 and 184.
Max Ophüls: 72.
Jean Renoir: 34, 35 and 78.
Roberto Rossellini: 37.
Jacques Tati: 83.

A selection of critical articles by Truffaut

THE EARLY YEARS

Cahiers du Cinéma, 31, January 1954: 'Une certain tendance du cinéma français'.
Cahiers du Cinéma, 91, January 1959: On the death of André Bazin.
Arts, 509, 30 March 1955: 'La crise d'ambition du cinéma français'.
Arts, 517, 25 May 1955: Cayatte and the script-writers.
Arts, 523, 6 July 1955: On critics.
Arts, 535, 28 September 1955: The script-writers' cinema.
Arts, 598, 19 December 1956: 1956 retrospective.
Arts, 619, 15 May 1957: Cannes 1957.
Arts, 652, 8 January 1958: New directors.
Arts, 687, 9 September 1958: *Les Amants* and *En Cas de Malheur*.
Arts, 697, 19 November 1958: On the death of André Bazin.

ON FILM-MAKERS

Jacques Becker: France-Observateur, 516, 24 March 1960.
Jean-Luc Godard: Les Lettres Françaises, 1174, 16 March 1967.
Ernst Lubitsch: Cahiers du Cinéma, 198, February 1968.
Jean Renoir: Le Monde, 7158, 18 January 1968.

ON ACTORS:

Charles Aznavour: Cinémonde, 1343, 5 May 1960.
Jean-Paul Belmondo: Unifrance, 369, 1 February 1969; Télérama, 966, 16 February 1969.
Jean-Claude Brialy: Programme du Théâtre Marigny ('La Puce à l'oreille')
Julie Christie: Arts-Loisirs, 53, 28 September 1966.
Catherine Deneuve: Unifrance, 370, 15 February 1969; Télérama, 996, 16 February 1969.
Marie Dubois: Programme du Théâtre Antoine ('Jessica').
Françoise Dorléac: Cahiers du Cinéma, 200–1, April–May 1968.

ON FILMS

Citizen Kane: L'Express, 441, 26 November 1959.
Le Pistonné: L'Express, 979, 13 April 1970.
Le Testament d'Orphée: Cahiers du Cinéma, 152, February 1964.
Le Vieil Homme et l'enfant: Le Nouvel Observateur.
Verboten: France-Observateur, 521, 28 April 1960; 121, 8 March 1967.
Vivre sa vie: L'Avant-scène du Cinéma, 19, 15 October 1962.
See also Lui, 1 and 2, November and December 1963.

TAKING SIDES

L'Affaire Vadim: France-Observateur, 555, 22 December 1960.
L'Agonie de la Nouvelle Vague n'est pas pour demain: Arts, 848, 20 December 1961.
L'Antimémoire Courte: Combat, 7334, 12 February 1968.
La Résistible Ascension de Pierre Barbin: Combat, 7338, 16 February 1968.
Toujours la Cinémathèque: Combat, 7362, 15 March 1968.
Vive 'Glenariff'!: Le Monde, 17 October 1969.

ON CINEASTES

André Bazin: Arts, 697, 19 November 1958.
Jean-Luc Godard: Seghers, Paris 1963, pp. 164-70.
Roberto Rossellini: Seghers, Paris 1961, pp. 199-205.
Georges Sadoul: Les Lettres Françaises, 1204, 18 October 1967.
Sur le cinéma américain: Cahiers du Cinéma, 150 and 151, December 1963 and January 1964.

BOOKS

Ce n'est qu'un début. Philippe Labro. Special edition, Editionet Publications Premières, 2. Denoël, Paris 1968, pp. 148–51 (Le Cinéma: François Truffaut raconte).
Le Cinéma selon Alfred Hitchcock. Robert Laffont. Paris 1967. (Hitchcock. Simon & Schuster, New York 1967; Secker & Warburg, London 1968.)